What Others Have Said.....

"One of the most meaningful times in life is when we gather around God's word for life change. Whether individually or corporately it is always time well spent. *Beyond Blessed* is an incredible way to do just that. Marsha Taylor's verse by verse look at Ephesians combines interesting truths for our minds and deep motivation for our hearts. I have had the joy of being Marsha's pastor and have known her entire family well for almost two decades. The Taylor family is the real deal! Grab a copy, a few friends, a cup of coffee and dig into the gold of Ephesians Marsha has mined out. I can assure you she will lead you to a place through this study that you will be - *Beyond Blessed!*"

— **Gregg Matte**, *Pastor of Houston's First Baptist Church, Houston, Texas*

"*Beyond Blessed* gives insightful foundational Truths that every believer needs to understand in living an empowering abundant life! My dear friend, Marsha, guides us all into the undeniable presence of God through the application of the Spiritual Truths found in Ephesians. I promise you a transformed, blessed life is awaiting you as you go through this amazing study!"

— **Mary Ann Bridgwater**, *President and Founder of Pray the Word Ministries*

"The study of Ephesians: *Beyond Blessed* is a labor of love from a serious, lifelong student. Marsha is a humble servant of Jesus Christ who embodies the rare combination of childlike faith and mature obedience in her teaching and daily living. She takes you deep into the treasures of Scripture while providing the tools to help you navigate difficult passages with ease. Whether you are a seeker curious about Jesus or a seasoned disciple, this study will cause the many blessings of God to fall fresh on your soul."

— **Christi Smith**, *Director of Women's Ministry at Houston First Baptist Church, Houston, Texas*

"Marsha is a gifted Bible teacher and speaker. She has been leading Bible studies for many years and has spent many hours studying the Word of God In order to clearly communicate the truths of His Word to the women she teaches. Her teaching reveals a deep love for the Lord and a passion to communicate His truths so others will know the Lord in deeper ways."

— **Toma Knight**, *Associate Pastor's Wife & Bible teacher at Lakeview Baptist Church, Auburn, Alabama*

"The *Beyond Blessed* study is so refreshing. Because of God's grace, I am sealed and secure in Christ. The study allowed me to pour through scripture each day, apply that scripture to my daily life, and be reminded of how much God loves me. It reinforces that as a follower of Jesus Christ I really am *Beyond Blessed!* As a women's Bible study leader, facilitating this study was easily adaptable to my church group. We downloaded the *Beyond Blessed* videos and used the group study questions and guides available on the Fresh Surrender website. We found the additional study questions thought-provoking, as they opened avenues for additional discussion and seeking answers from God's Word. As a facilitator, the ease with which this study flowed, and the growth seen in the women who attended is something that warms my heart. Whether an individual, a few friends in a homegroup, or church Bible study class, I recommend this study to everyone."

— **Maureen Everett**, *Women's Bible Study Leader, Marble Falls, Texas*

"The *Beyond Blessed* study touched my heart - I loved it! It didn't just inform and educate; it gave me tools to help my walk and to be strong."

— **Sandra Cobb**, *Beyond Blessed Study, Houston, Texas*

"What a true blessing! God spoke in so many ways through *Beyond Blessed!* Marsha created it, but God personalized it to everyone who participated. How special!"

— **Charity Tolbert**, *Beyond Blessed Study, Houston, Texas*

MARSHA TAYLOR

Beyond Blessed

An 8-Week Study of the Book of Ephesians

Beyond Blessed

An 8-Week Study of the Book of Ephesians

Copyright © 2022 by Marsha Taylor

Published by Lucid Books in Houston, TX
www.lucidbooks.com

ISBN 978-1-63296-523-3 (paperback)
ISBN 978-1-63296-524-0 (ebook)

Special Sales: Most Lucid Books titles are available in special quantity discounts. Custom imprinting or excerpting can also be done to fit special needs.
For standard bulk orders, go to www.lucidbooksbulk.com.
For specialty press or large orders, contact Lucid Books at info@lucidbooks.com.

Special Thanks

First and foremost, I am overwhelmed at the sacrifice of Jesus on my behalf, grateful for His blessing, and honored to serve Him as my Savior, my Lord, and my very Life.

I am so grateful for the encouragement of the following friends and family who have listened to me, challenged me, and supported me in this endeavor:

- To my girls, Catherine and Caroline—Thank you for listening to me, for supporting me, and for loving me. I am blessed to be your mom. And Will, I'm grateful that you are part of our family, and I appreciate your insight.
- To Maureen—Thank you for being a great sounding board, proofreader, and amazing lifelong friend. You are my sharpening iron.
- To Melissa—Thank you for serving at my side in ministry, for hours of proofreading, and your support and encouragement.
- To Karen—Thank you for believing in me long before I could see God's equipping.
- To Denise, Jamie, Leslie, and Shannon—Thank you for your support, help, insight, and willingness to speak the truth in love.
- To Ryan and the Indie-Pepper Creative—Thank you for all your help in graphic and video design.
- And to my best friend and amazing husband, David – Thank you for loving me, supporting me, and praying for me. I am honored to be your wife. Other than my salvation, you are the greatest gift God has bestowed on me.

Table of Contents

Purpose

How "Beyond Blessed" is Designed

Beyond Blessed is designed for daily study in God's Word. Each lesson covers a specific passage of scripture from Ephesians and divides the focal passage into five days of study. Ideally, you should complete one lesson per week. My desire is for you to search your Bible to find deeper meaning and personal application of the truths in these lessons. The questions are designed for you to answer with your own thoughts and ideas from the scripture and not simply write the verse verbatim from your Bible.

I have written the study in a conversational style, which may be different than other studies you have done. I want each reader and student to feel they have someone by their side as they are studying. If you are a person who likes to read the scripture chapters in order, please know that we skip around some since the workbook chapters are organized by topic rather than verse order, but we will study all of Ephesians.

> Each day's lesson in the workbook is estimated to take 20–40 minutes, and the entire lesson should take 1–2 hours. The questions use the English Standard Version (ESV) of the Bible. If you are using another version and do not understand a question or how to answer it, please check the ESV for clarity.

I believe that the time you spend in God's Word will be extremely beneficial. **Hebrews 4:12** tells us that His Word is living and active, so each time you look at scripture, God is going to speak to your heart to bring you encouragement, correction, or instruction. Oh, friend, that can be a specific word about something He wants to do or change in your life, something about the situation or circumstances you are facing, something about His character and His love for you, or something all together new. Whatever He wants to say, it is thrilling to hear the very words of God speaking to your soul.

So dig in! Enjoy the depth of each verse you look up. My desire in writing this study is to take you into the Old and New Testaments to see for yourself that God is the same yesterday, today, and forever, and to learn how all scripture works together beautifully to glorify God and point us to His Son, Jesus.

Do your best to complete the lessons without consulting a commentary for assistance. Commentaries can be excellent tools for additional study, but it is more meaningful when you find the answer in His Word. Pray, and ask God to help you find the answer to a question you are struggling with or is challenging to you.

God wants you to learn from Him and His Word, and it is thrilling when He teaches you.

Resources

To enhance your study, there are teaching videos that accompany each week's lesson. If you are able to work through this book in a group setting with your friends or at your church, discussion questions are also available.

Both resources can be downloaded at www.freshsurrender.org.

For Leaders

If you are interested in leading a group in your home, community, or church, please visit www.freshsurrender.org for additional materials to download free of charge.

Small group discussion questions, listening guides to accompany the video teaching, and administrative materials to help facilitate a class are also available on the website.

If you are interested in teaching the material rather than using the video content and facilitating a group, please know that is thrilling to me. I am praying that teachers will find the workbook content complementary to their teaching.

Preface

There is a story about an undernourished boy who was found on a city street and taken to a hospital. After the nurse bathed him and dressed him, she put him to bed and brought him a dinner tray that included a large glass of milk. The boy's eyes lit up when he reached for the milk, but then he paused and looked up at the nurse. He asked, "May I drink all of it?" At that moment, she realized that in this little boy's experience, there was never enough milk to go around. "Yes," she replied, "drink it all!"

I am so excited that you are choosing to study the book of Ephesians. It records the vast riches available to you, and rest assured, there is more than enough to go around! Sadly, too often Christians do not drink deeply enough of the riches and abundance that is theirs in Christ Jesus. Too often in the spiritual sense, we are malnourished children sitting at the banquet table of the King of kings. Oh, that in these next weeks we would learn to drink deeply and eat heartily from the abundance God has provided!

As we embark together on this journey through the book of Ephesians, I pray that you will come to see how deeply God loves you, that you will know He accepts you, and that you will be assured that in Him you are worthy of all the blessings He pours out on your life. God has given you so much in Jesus Christ. As His child now and for all eternity, you are beyond blessed!

But as God's blessed children, we are expected to go beyond our blessing and live in a way that is worthy of our calling as His children. This journey will not only help you see the riches you have received in Christ but will also show you how you can use those rich gifts to bless others and glorify God through practical living.

Introduction

As we begin this journey into the wonderful book of Ephesians, it is my prayer that God will truly speak to your heart, that your love for the Lord will deepen, and that you will grow in your relationship with Him and learn much about His immense love for you. Dig into your study questions, and seek to know Him better, but also realize that you are deeply known by your heavenly Father. Ephesians is His love letter to you. No matter your background, your bank account, your mistakes, your failures, your successes, or your insecurities—no matter what—God lavishes His love upon you, blessing heaped upon blessing. And He lays it out through Paul in this beautiful epistle to the Ephesians.

I want you to be bold, to ask God daily to let His Word not just increase in your knowledge of Him but also to allow it to invade your heart. I understand that this can be hard, especially when we have been wounded. Please know that I, too, have been wounded in the past, but I want to have victory over those past hurts and learn to live in freedom—a freedom that has been given to you and me by the power of the cross and by Jesus' victory over death!

So let's jump in with some quick basic facts about the book of Ephesians, its writer, and the city of Ephesus.

The Book of Ephesians

The book of Ephesians was written by Paul, and many consider it to be his masterpiece. It tells of the remarkable blessing God has given to all who have found salvation in Jesus Christ. This beautiful book of the Bible expounds on the great riches given to us by God, our future inheritance held in heaven for us, and the responsibility we have to lead lives that reflect the thankfulness and gratitude we have to God for our gifts and salvation. I believe that until we fully understand all we have been given by God in Christ, we cannot fully live for Him and experience the freedom He offers us through His Son. The book of Ephesians is very logically arranged. The first three chapters of the book focus on doctrine and theology, and the last three chapters focus on behavior and practical living.

The Writer of Ephesians – Paul

The book of Ephesians was a letter Paul wrote to the Christians in the church located in the city of Ephesus. Paul had visited Ephesus on a missionary journey, remaining in the city for about two years, founding the first Christian church there, and serving as the pastor. Paul wrote this letter during his imprisonment in Rome around AD 62 to encourage the people of this church.

If you don't know much about this great man of God, his original name was Saul. He was a Roman citizen and of Jewish lineage, of the tribe of Benjamin, and most likely named after Israel's first king. He was well educated in Jerusalem at the finest rabbinical school. A religious leader of his day, Saul was an outstanding scholar and member of the Sanhedrin, the ruling Jewish council in Jerusalem.

Regarding Christianity, Saul was vehemently against all followers of Jesus and was possibly the most anti-Christian leader in Judaism. He passionately hated those who followed Christ, persecuting and killing many of them. Ironically, during one of his campaigns to arrest a group of Christians, God struck him blind along the way and dramatically brought him to faith in Jesus Christ as the Messiah.

As a new convert to the way of Jesus Christ, Saul took on the new name of 'Paul'. He studied his new faith and began a ministry that would change the world. During his ministry, he traveled in Asia Minor and Europe where he made it his practice to live in various communities where he taught people and converted them to Christianity. He also established churches in those areas. When he moved to a new city, he often wrote letters to those established churches to encourage them, addressing areas of confusion about their faith and correcting any actions or attitudes that did not honor Christ. Thirteen of these letters are included in the New Testament.

As a powerful evangelist for the gospel of Jesus Christ, Paul frequently angered the Jewish religious leaders as well as civil authorities. He was frequently running for his life and was imprisoned several times. While the details of his death are uncertain, most historians believe he was beheaded in Rome during the reign of the insanely cruel emperor Nero.

Ephesus

The city of Ephesus was in the heart of the Roman Empire. It had a population of approximately 350,000 people and was a leading city, second in importance to Rome. Ephesus was a great cultural and religious center and a beautiful coastal city where Roman emperors vacationed. It was the site of the Temple of Diana, one of the Seven Wonders of the Ancient World. Paul visited the city of Ephesus on two separate missionary journeys.

He lived in Ephesus for approximately two years. While there, he not only founded the church but also served as its pastor, which means the church at Ephesus received more direct teaching from Paul than any other church. The church at Ephesus was large and influential. Paul wrote the letter to the Ephesians about 10 years after leaving Ephesus.

PAUL'S INTRODUCTION
— EPHESIANS 1:1-2 —

PAUL, AN APOSTLE OF CHRIST JESUS BY THE WILL OF GOD, TO THE SAINTS WHO ARE IN EPHESUS, AND ARE FAITHFUL IN CHRIST JESUS: GRACE TO YOU AND PEACE FROM GOD OUR FATHER AND THE LORD JESUS CHRIST.

Paul begins his letters with a formal greeting, telling who the letter is from and for whom the letter is intended. In this case, Paul refers to himself as an apostle, which is an interesting title. Originally, Jesus chose 12 disciples who are also referred to as apostles. To be an apostle, a person had to receive his calling directly from the lips of Jesus Christ. While Paul did not meet Jesus before His death, he did see the risen Christ along the road to a city called Damascus. During this conversion experience, Paul was given authority by God to preach, perform miracles, and establish churches. (To learn more about the conversion of Saul/Paul, see **Acts 9:1–31**.)

In **Ephesians 1:1**, Paul states that this letter is written to the "saints who are in Ephesus." Remember, Paul had lived in Ephesus for two years and had established the church in the city, serving as its pastor. He knew these people well and called them saints. The Greek word for saint means one who is separated or holy, one who has been set aside for God's sole use.

Do you realize that those who are in Christ today are also called saints? As Christians, we have been set apart for God's sole use, just as those in the days of Paul in Ephesus. It is a beautiful calling, but I think it's one we sometimes misunderstand since we often equate being a saint with being perfect. Oh, friend! That is not what this word means! I believe the concept of being set aside and called holy is best seen in a time much earlier than Paul—in the days of Moses when he led the Israelites out of bondage in Egypt.

In the years after Moses led the children of God out of Egypt, they wandered around in the wilderness, pitching tents, taking them down, setting the tents up again, and walking around no telling how many times. One of the tents they continually set up and took down was the Tabernacle, a very holy place where the people worshiped God. Inside were the holy items used in worship, including metal bowls and clay pieces that I'm sure had been dinged a few times in all the moving. Maybe they had a chip or a crack in them, a little dent, or perhaps a film of dust. These pieces were not considered holy because they were fine and nice but because they were intended for God's use. Likewise, we may get a little beat up along our journey, but we are still holy. We are still called saints, not because of the way we act but because of our position in Christ. We belong to God to be used by God.

Paul also offers grace and peace to the readers. Grace is the Greek word *charis*, a customary Greek greeting, while the word peace is the Hebrew word *shalom*, a customary Jewish greeting. By simply using these two words, Paul is welcoming all people—whether Jew or Greek—to read his letter. In addition, grace is God's undeserved favor to a sinner that comes in the form of complete forgiveness of sin and the granting of eternal life. Peace is the result of that amazing gift of love. Very simply, grace covers your sin, and peace covers your guilt. We need to bathe in these two truths—God's grace and peace—daily! What joy in knowing our sin is covered completely by His grace and that we can rest in His peace as He removes all our guilt!

Already in just two verses, we are beginning to see how special we are to God. As His children, we are holy saints set apart to be used by Him and given complete forgiveness of our sin by His grace, and we are at peace with God. And we are just getting started! The next verses in our study are some of my favorites in all Scripture. As you prepare for Lesson One, take a moment to read **Ephesians 1:3–14** in its entirety. In the original Greek language, in which Paul wrote this letter, it was one very long, run-on sentence. Our modern translations have included punctuation for clarity and to help us understand Paul's meaning better, but it is so beautiful to read the entire passage together and see blessing heaped upon blessing.

LESSON ONE

Spiritual Blessings

— EPHESIANS 1:3-14 —

Looking at the first chapter of Ephesians, we learn of the lavish spiritual blessings that have been poured out in abundance on all believers. Understanding the principle of being "in Christ" is especially important because it is the key to understanding our identity in Jesus. It is our identity in Him that allows us to walk spiritually in freedom, to quit trying to perform for God's and other people's approval, and to have deep and meaningful relationships with other people. Knowing our worth and value to God allows us to stop working in our own efforts and start living in God's strength, allowing Him to work in and through us.

As you work through the questions included in this lesson, try to complete each one using only your Bible. Commentaries can be a great reference to understand God's Word better, but they are filled with human words and ideas. As an exercise to grow in your faith, ask God to speak to you through His Word and reveal the answers to you through His Word alone. If you are struggling, use additional translations of the Bible to help gain perspective. While there are many ways to use other translations, a great resource in seeing multiple translations online is www.biblegateway.com. (The questions have been written using the English Standard Version.)

> In preparation for this lesson, read Ephesians 1:3–14, and circle in your Bible or note in the margin the number of occurrences of the words "in Him" and "in Christ."

What Does It Mean to Be "in Christ"?

We are all born into a family. Your family shares a gene pool, unique family traits, and maybe even a bit of property or a farmhouse that has been passed down through the generations. We are also born into a spiritual family that began with Adam and Eve. So not only are we physically in the Smith family or the Brown family but we are also born spiritually "in Adam." Being born in Adam also comes with shared traits—a sinful nature and a life heading toward eternal separation from God.

When we accept Jesus Christ as our Savior, we are born again and adopted spiritually into the family of God. We are no longer in Adam but have been accepted into God's family and are spiritually "in Christ." Our sins have been forgiven, and we take on the righteousness of Christ. We now share in the inheritance God has secured for us in heaven.

To further illustrate what it means to be "in Christ," let's consider the idea of being voted into a political position such as a congressional representative. All the power, privileges, and responsibilities of that position are yours. You have a place there. You are accepted there. You got there by required means, so you are worthy to be there.

The same applies to being in Christ.
All His holiness, goodness, glory, power, and wealth are yours.
You are accepted; you have a place, and you are worthy to be called His.
You are in Christ.

DAY 1
— READ *EPHESIANS 1:3* —

The word *blessed* in our English translations comes from the Greek word *eulogeo*, which means "to speak well of." This Greek word is the root of our English word *eulogy*. This passage contains several variants of this root word.

1   Read **Ephesians 1:3.** Who is blessed (or praised) in this verse?

_____

_____

_____

2   The word **blessed** occurs two times in **Ephesians 1:3**, and each occurrence has a different meaning. The first instance—"**Blessed** be the God and Father of our Lord Jesus Christ" is a slight variation of the base Greek word **eulogeo**. When used in Scripture, this word only refers to God since it carries the idea of inherent worth.

In searching the verses below, what are some of the ways God is worthy to be praised?

Isaiah 45:5, 7, 12

_____

_____

_____

1 Chronicles 29:11–12

_____

_____

_____

Psalm 147:5

_____

_____

_____

Zephaniah 3:17

_____

_____

_____

3 In addition, we also see the relationship between **God the Father** and the **Lord Jesus Christ** at the beginning of **Ephesians 1:3**.

How is this relationship represented in the following verses?

Matthew 3:16–17

_____

_____

_____

Matthew 16:15–17

_____

_____

_____

2 John 1:3

_____

_____

_____

4 The second occurrence of the word _blessed_ is in the latter part of **Ephesians 1:3**, which says, "who has blessed us in Christ with every spiritual blessing in the heavenly places." The meaning of the Greek word for this use of _blessed_ means God is speaking well of you and is working in your life to bring you into the desired relationship with Him.

According to this verse, who has God blessed?

_____

_____

_____

_____

_____

_____

5 To what extent did God go to bring you into a relationship with Him?

John 3:16

_____

_____

_____

Romans 8:3–4

_____

_____

_____

Galatians 4:4–5

_____

_____

_____

1 John 4:8–10

_____

_____

_____

6 Take a few moments to reflect on what God has shown you in today's study. Write some of the ways you are thankful and how He is worthy of praise.

_____

_____

_____

_____

DAY 2
— READ *EPHESIANS 1:4* —

Today's verses will cover some of the most debated concepts in Christianity. These concepts will be explored in this lesson, but they are still somewhat of a mystery. If you do not fully understand them, you are not alone! We will not fully understand the mind of God until we are face to face with Him in heaven. In our reading of Scripture, we will come to confusing and difficult passages. Don't let any confusion or nonunderstanding of complicated passages discourage you. Some of the greatest minds in Christian history have devoted themselves to studying these passages, and yet there is no clear understanding. Ask God to help you better understand His Word. Also, know that mystery surrounding these concepts will remain.

1   Read **Ephesians 1:4.** Who is blessed (or praised) in this verse?

_____

_____

_____

2   What was the purpose or result of His choosing you?

_____

_____

_____

3   How is this further expanded in **Psalm 139:13–18**? These verses record the love God has for you and the care He has taken to plan for you. In your Bible, circle any words that demonstrate His love for you in these verses.

If you are uncomfortable writing in your Bible, you may record them below.

_____

_____

_____

_____

4 Look up the words *holy* and *blameless* in a dictionary, and record their definitions.

Holy

_____

_____

_____

Blameless

_____

_____

_____

5 How does God work on our behalf to make us holy and blameless?

Colossians 1:21–22

_____

_____

_____

2 Corinthians 5:21

_____

_____

_____

Philippians 3:9

_____

_____

_____

6 As you looked into God's Word today, what did He show you that was particularly meaningful? Why not thank God for His amazing love toward you and what He is showing you through His Word?

_____

_____

_____

_____

_____

ELECTION *versus* FREE WILL

The doctrine of election states that God chose us before He created the universe, so His salvation is wholly of His grace and not based on anything we have done. We are chosen in Christ and not in ourselves. We are chosen for a purpose, which is stated in Ephesians 1:4, to be holy and without blame. Warren Wiersbe said, "The mystery of divine sovereignty and human responsibility will never be solved in this life. Both are taught in the Bible. Both are true, and both are essential."[1]

Maybe the best way to understand these principles is through illustration, specifically the betrothal process in biblical times. In ancient times, a father selected a bride for his son, and then the father of the groom and the father of the bride met. These fathers settled on the amount the groom would have to pay the father for his daughter's hand. Once that amount was paid, the groom planned a day to go to the bride's home and ask her to marry him.

On the appointed day, the groom went to the girl's house, stood at her door, and knocked. If she opened the door and let him in, the two would have a meal together; however, the potential bride did have the right to say no and not open the door. If she said yes, then following the meal, the groom would present the girl with an engagement ring—a guarantee that he would be back for her. He would then leave and build a home for them to live in and return once the father of the groom said the house was ready, and the marriage would follow.

Do you hear "election"?
The father of the groom chooses the wife to be.
Do you hear "free will"?
She had the right to say no and the responsibility to open the door.

"God's sovereign election and man's exercise of responsibility in choosing Jesus Christ seem opposite and irreconcilable truths—and from our limited human perspective, they are opposite and irreconcilable. . . . since the problem cannot be resolved by our finite minds, the result is always to compromise one truth in favor of the other or to weaken both in trying to take a position somewhere between them. We should let the antinomy remain, believing both truths completely and leaving the harmonizing of them to God."[2]

—*John MacArthur*

DAY 3
— READ *EPHESIANS 1:5-10* —

Like election and free will, predestination is also a hard principle to understand. *Predestination* means "to define, to mark out, to set apart," and it only applies to those who are believers in Christ Jesus. So where election seems to refer to people, predestination seems to refer to purpose.

1 **Ephesians 1:5** tells us that we have been predestined for adoption as sons (and daughters) into His family. What does **Romans 8:14–16** say about adoption?

_____

_____

In Ephesians 1:6, the word "blessed" is used again. But according to the Greek, this word is not the same or a derivative of the word we looked at on Day 1. Instead, it is a variant of the word for grace. This word means "to make acceptable, make lovely and deserving of love."[3] Do you hear that you are acceptable, lovely, and deserving of God's love? What a blessing!

2 Read **Ephesians 1:7.** Using a dictionary, define the following words:

Redemption

_____

_____

_____

_____
_____
_____

3   In Christ, we have been redeemed by His blood. What do you learn about redemption from the following verses?

Hebrews 9:14, 22

_____
_____
_____

Galatians 3:13–14

_____
_____
_____

Galatians 4:4–5

_____
_____
_____

4   God's forgiveness is available to everyone. No matter what a person has done, from telling a little white lie to the worst imaginable offense, they can be forgiven. Jesus' blood has the power to wash all things clean for those who are in Christ.

What do the following verses reveal about God's forgiveness?

Hebrews 9:14, 22

_____
_____
_____

1 John 1:8–9

_____
_____
_____

5

Ephesians 1:9 tells us that God has made the mystery of His will known to us, which is set forth in Jesus. Sometimes we can feel that many things of God are a mystery to us, but God wants to make Himself known and wants us to understand that salvation is found in no other name but Jesus.

What do you learn about the mystery of God from the following verses?

The mystery of the Gentiles sharing in the promises God made to the Jews:

Ephesians 3:6

_____

_____

Colossians 1:27

_____

_____

The mystery of redemption through Jesus:

1 Timothy 3:16

_____

_____

Colossians 2:2–3

_____

_____

Look again at **Ephesians 1:9**. After studying the verses on God's mystery, what do you believe is the mystery Paul is speaking of in Ephesians?

_____

_____

_____

6

In our study today, we have looked at the mystery of God—the gospel of Jesus Christ. Jesus came into the world—God in flesh—and died in your place for your sin. In Him, you have redemption and forgiveness, and purpose. Why not thank God for all He has done for you?

_____

_____

_____

DAY 4
— READ *EPHESIANS 1:11-12* —

Once again, we see the designation of being "in Christ" in these verses today, and we see the concept of predestination again. These verses also tell us another spiritual blessing we have in Jesus—sharing in the inheritance God has stored in heaven for Jesus. God considers you His child, adopted into His family, and He plans to share His riches with you for eternity.

1 According to the verses below, what are some of the things our inheritance consists of?

Ephesians 1:3

_____

_____

_____

2 Peter 1:3–4

_____

_____

_____

2 Read **1 Peter 1:3–5**, and answer the following questions:

• How have we come to be born again?

_____

_____

_____

_____

_____

_____

_____

- Describe our inheritance.

_____

_____

_____

_____

- Where is it kept for us?

_____

_____

_____

- How is it protected?

_____

_____

_____

- When will it be received?

_____

_____

_____

3

Not only do you have an inheritance waiting for you in heaven but you also have a purpose here on earth. Isn't it amazing? God—Who created everything, Who owns everything, Who empowers everything, Who is more powerful and wise than we can imagine and more loving than we can fathom—this God chose you before the world came into being. And He chose you to be His—not His friend, His acquaintance, or His servant, but His son or daughter. And He has given you a purpose, established (predestined) for you before time began.

How do the following verses explain this purpose?

Romans 8:29

_____

_____

_____

Ephesians 2:10

_____

_____

_____

4 **Titus 3:3–7** is a beautiful summary of the work God does from salvation to eternal life. Write these verses below, inserting your name into the sentences.

_____

_____

_____

5 Looking at the previous question, write a prayer of thanksgiving for all God has done for you.

_____

_____

_____

_____

DAY 5
— READ *EPHESIANS 1:13-14* —

Today we are going to focus on the work of the Holy Spirit. Upon salvation, the Holy Spirit comes to live in you as God's deposit. (Think of it in terms of a major purpose such as a home. You put down a deposit, which secures your future purchase.) When you accept Jesus as your Savior, the Holy Spirit is "deposited" into your life and secures all the promises God has made to you for your future home in heaven and eternal inheritance. The Holy Spirit also does a great work in you and through you, as we will study today.

1 According to **Ephesians 1:13–14**, what did the Ephesians do upon hearing the word of truth? Upon believing, what else occurred? What do you learn about the Holy Spirit?

_____

_____

_____

_____

2 Read **Romans 10:9–10** and **Galatians 2:16**. According to these verses, how does someone come to faith in Jesus Christ?

_____

_____

_____

_____

3 Coming to a saving faith in Jesus is as simple as accepting His invitation. It doesn't depend on your works. You don't have to be good enough or clean up your life for Him, and going to church doesn't make you a Christian. The way to Jesus is to recognize that you have sin in your life and then accept His death on the cross as your payment for the debt you owe to God for that sin. You simply recognize your need for Jesus to save you and ask Him to do so.

You ask His forgiveness and ask Him to come into your life. The moment you do, the Holy Spirit enters your life and secures your life in eternity. If you have never accepted the gift of salvation, please consider asking Him to save you now.

SEALING OF THE HOLY SPIRIT

When I was a little girl, I had a stationery set that came with assorted wax candles and a metal stamp with an "M" on it. To seal my letters, I lit the candle and melted some wax on the envelope. I then pressed the metal stamp into the hot wax to create a seal with my initial. While I did not realize it at the time, that was a very regal thing to do! In ancient times, letters and official decrees were sealed in the same manner with a signet ring. This seal would identify the document and by whose authority the decree was sent.

Likewise, we have been sealed with the Holy Spirit. It signifies whose authority we are under and carries the promise of fulfillment by the King of kings.

4

What is the work of the Holy Spirit?

Psalm 143:10

_____

_____

_____

John 14:26

_____

_____

_____

John 15:26

_____

_____

_____

Romans 8:26

_____

_____

_____

2 Timothy 1:14

_____

_____

_____

5 Reflection: Look back at **Ephesians 1:1–14**, and reflect on all you have studied.

- What has been something new God has shown you about Himself or His Word?

_____

_____

_____

- In what ways have you been challenged to walk more deeply in your relationship with Him?

_____

_____

_____

- How has studying His Word made a difference in your life this week?

_____
_____
_____

Concluding Thoughts

It is beyond my comprehension that the God of the universe speaks well of me and finds me worthy of blessing. I can so easily see my mistakes, my faults, and my failures, and I have a running list of all the ways I feel I have disappointed my family, my friends, and the people at my work. I know I have disappointed God in so many ways. But what God sees when He looks at me is none of this—none of the mistakes, none of the failures, and none of the faults, because I am a saint, holy and set apart for His purposes.

Oh, friend! For those of us who are in Christ, this is *not* what God sees when He looks at you either! He sees a magnificent and wonderful person. You are His child. He sees you as holy and righteous because your faults and mistakes—your sins—have been covered by the blood of Jesus Christ and completely forgiven and removed. You are worthy, not because of anything you have done or not done but because you are in Him. Your Father God speaks well of you!

God has also poured out His blessings on your life. Yes, these are blessings that are held for you in heaven, but they are also blessings we can experience now. When life seems to be more than we can bear, when we have struggles and difficulties, when we need to know God is right there with us, He gives us an overflowing abundance of His blessing at our disposal anytime. Just in these few verses, we have seen that we are:

SPOKEN WELL OF BY GOD
HOLY
BLAMELESS
ADOPTED INTO THE FAMILY OF GOD
REDEEMED
FORGIVEN
GIVEN A PURPOSE
RECIPIENTS OF THE RICHES OF GOD'S GRACE
UNDERSTANDING OF THE MYSTERY OF THE GOSPEL

In addition, God also has given us an inheritance and a promise, which includes every spiritual blessing in Christ. If you know Jesus as your Savior, you have been given the Holy Spirit as a *deposit*, a guarantee that God is holding your inheritance in heaven for you. I like the literal translation of the word deposit in **Ephesians 1:13** from the Greek. It is the same word for an engagement ring. Our guarantee—our sealing by the Holy Spirit, our engagement ring—is very significant. It speaks of a finished transaction. In biblical days, once the ring was placed on a girl's finger, it took the legal action of a divorce to end the union. Once a girl took the ring, it was a done deal—a finished transaction.

The guarantee also implies ownership. Just as the wedding ring on my finger shows everyone I belong to my husband, David, and the ring on his finger shows the world he is mine, the deposit of the Holy Spirit in us reminds us that we belong to God.

Isn't it clear to you by now? God is crazy about you! He lavishes His love upon you, desires an intimate relationship with you, and pours out His blessings on your life. We are *Beyond Blessed* in Jesus! And Paul is not done recounting all our blessings in his letter to the Ephesians. The next two chapters in Paul's letter continue to show us how special and loved we are in the eyes of our Father.

Additional Notes

_____

_____

_____

_____

_____

_____

_____

_____

_____

_____

_____

_____

_____

_____

LESSON TWO

Saved by Grace

— EPHESIANS 2:1–3:13 —

In Ephesians 1, Paul beautifully told the saints about their new identity now that they are in Christ, but he starts chapter two with a stern reminder of who they were before finding salvation in Jesus. Paul says that at one time they were dead in their trespasses. The word dead means just that—spiritually unable to understand and appreciate spiritual things. We can do nothing to please God. Basically, all of us were walking corpses!

In **Romans 7:18–19 (NLT)**, Paul says, "I want to do what is right, but I can't. I want to do what is good, but I don't. I don't want to do what is wrong, but I do it anyway." While most of us never desire to be disobedient to God, while we are still on this earth, we will be prone to sin. The Bible often refers to this sinful nature as "being in the flesh." And our flesh is weak.

When we are living in the flesh, we will be susceptible to:

- **The power of the world.** This is the pressure to conform and look like the world and those in it. It's the pressure to wear the right thing, live in a nice house, and have the right set of friends. It is also the pressure to compromise our morals and behavior. We cut corners, miss church, or tell little white lies—and suddenly we don't recognize ourselves anymore.

- **The power of the prince of the air.** This is the influence of Satan. While he doesn't know our thoughts, Satan is pretty good at accurately guessing how we are feeling and what we are thinking. After all, he has known mankind for thousands of years. He uses lies to get us to believe we are less than God says and that we should walk in guilt over what we have done wrong in our lives. But Jesus' death not only brings forgiveness of sin but also removes your guilt. Don't let Satan lie to you. You are freed from guilt by the cross.

- **The power of the flesh.** Just by being born, we all inherit a sinful nature from our ancient father, Adam, which makes us desire to control our bodies and minds. Sadly, it is in our nature to disobey God.

We have all come from the place of being spiritually dead. We have all missed the mark, and because of our sin, we were dead. Tell me, what can a dead body do? Nothing! If you have any idea that you did something to help God in the salvation process, remember this: you were a corpse. You and I did nothing. God does it all! Warren Wiersbe states it this way: "The unbeliever is not sick; he is dead! He does not need resuscitation, he needs resurrection. All lost sinners are dead, and the only difference between one sinner and another is the state of decay. The lost derelict on skid row may be more decayed outwardly than the unsaved society leader, but both are dead in sin—and one corpse cannot be more dead than another!"[4]

Ephesians 2:1–22

From Death to Life

1 In the past you were dead because you sinned and fought against God. **2** You followed the ways of this world and obeyed the devil. He rules the world, and his spirit has power over everyone who doesn't obey God. **3** Once we were also ruled by the selfish desires of our bodies and minds. We had made God angry, and we were going to be punished like everyone else.

4-5 But God was merciful! We were dead because of our sins, but God loved us so much that he made us alive with Christ, and God's wonderful kindness is what saves you. **6** God raised us from death to life with Christ Jesus, and he has given us a place beside Christ in heaven. **7** God did this so that in the future world he could show how truly good and kind he is to us because of what Christ Jesus has done. **8** You were saved by faith in God, who treats us much better than we deserve. This is God's gift to you, and not anything you have done on your own. **9** It isn't something you have earned, so there is nothing you can brag about. **10** God planned for us to do good things and to live as he has always wanted us to live. That's why he sent Christ to make us what we are.

United by Christ

11 Don't forget that you are Gentiles. In fact, you used to be called "uncircumcised" by those who take pride in being circumcised. **12** At that time you did not know about Christ. You were foreigners to the people of Israel, and you had no part in the promises that God had made to them. You were living in this world without hope and without God, **13** and you were far from God. But Christ offered his life's blood as a sacrifice and brought you near God.

14 Christ has made peace between Jews and Gentiles, and he has united us by breaking down the wall of hatred that separated us. Christ gave his own body 15 to destroy the Law of Moses with all its rules and commands. He even brought Jews and Gentiles together as though we were only one person, when he united us in peace. 16 On the cross Christ did away with our hatred for each other. He also made peace between us and God by uniting Jews and Gentiles in one body. 17 Christ came and preached peace to you Gentiles, who were far from God, and peace to us Jews, who were near God. 18 And because of Christ, all of us can come to the Father by the same Spirit.

19 You Gentiles are no longer strangers and foreigners. You are citizens with everyone else who belongs to the family of God. 20 You are like a building with the apostles and prophets as the foundation and with Christ as the most important stone. 21 Christ is the one who holds the building together and makes it grow into a holy temple for the Lord. 22 And you are part of that building Christ has built as a place for God's own Spirit to live.

Ephesians 3:1–13

Paul's Mission to the Gentiles

1 Christ Jesus made me his prisoner, so that I could help you Gentiles. 2 You have surely heard about God's kindness in choosing me to help you. 3 In fact, this letter tells you a little about how God has shown me his mysterious ways. 4 As you read the letter, you will also find out how well I do understand the mystery about Christ. 5 No one knew about this mystery until God's Spirit told it to his holy apostles and prophets. 6 And the mystery is this: Because of Christ Jesus, the good news has given the Gentiles a share in the promises that God gave to the Jews. God has also let the Gentiles be part of the same body.

7 God treated me with kindness. His power worked in me, and it became my job to spread the good news. 8 I am the least important of all God's people. But God was kind and chose me to tell the Gentiles that because of Christ there are blessings that cannot be measured. 9 God, who created everything, wanted me to help everyone understand the mysterious plan that had always been hidden in his mind. 10 Then God would use the church to show the powers and authorities in the spiritual world that he has many different kinds of wisdom.

11 God did this according to his eternal plan. And he was able to do what he had planned because of all that Christ Jesus our Lord had done. 12 Christ now gives us courage and confidence, so that we can come to God by faith. 13 That's why you should not be discouraged when I suffer for you. After all, it will bring honor to you.

DAY 1
— READ *EPHESIANS 2:1-10* —

1 Read **Ephesians 2:1–3.** What do you learn about who you were in the past (before you came to know Jesus Christ as your personal Savior)?

_____

_____

_____

2 One of my favorite words in all of Scripture is, You may have been one thing in the past, "but God" did an amazing work through His grace. What do you learn in **Ephesians 2:4–6**?

_____

_____

_____

3 Why did God do these things? (See **Ephesians 2:7**)?

_____

_____

_____

4 **Ephesians 2:8–10** are verses that are often quoted and even memorized. What do you learn in these verses? (Use the ESV text below for your answer.)

"For by grace you have been saved through faith. And this is not your own doing; it is the gift of God, not a result of works, so that no one may boast. For we are his workmanship, created in Christ Jesus for good works, which God prepared beforehand, that we should walk in them."

_____

_____

_____

5 The purpose of our good works is not for salvation but so others will see that our lives are controlled by God and give Him glory. In **Titus 2**, there is a list of good works we can walk in and show others that we are His children by our actions. Read through this chapter, and record the actions you would like God to move and develop more in your life.

_____

_____

_____

6 As you reflect on all God has done for you and how your life should reflect your gratitude for His grace, what areas of your life do you want to give to God to better display His love to others?

_____

_____

_____

_____

"A famous actor was once the guest of honor at a social gathering where he received many requests to recite favorite excerpts from various literary works. An old preacher who happened to be there asked the actor to recite the Twenty-third Psalm. The actor agreed on the condition that the preacher would also recite it. The actor's recitation was beautifully intoned with great dramatic emphasis, for which he received lengthy applause. The preacher's voice was rough and broken from many years of preaching, and his diction was anything but polished. But when he finished there was not a dry eye in the room. When someone asked the actor what made the difference, he replied, 'I know the Psalm, but he knows the Shepherd.' Salvation does not come from knowing about the truth of Jesus Christ but from intimately knowing Christ Himself. This coming alive can be accomplished by the power of God because of His love and mercy."[5]

—John MacArthur

DAY 2
— READ EPHESIANS 2:11-13 —

Just as our section yesterday reminded us of who we once were before we came to salvation in Jesus Christ, our section today has the same reminder. And it also contains the wonderful words "but God." God did an amazing work in bringing us salvation; in addition, the work of Christ has brought us peace with God.

1 Read **Ephesians 2:11–12.** Write what you've learned about the Gentiles and the Jews under the column headings below:

GENTILES   **JEWS**

2 Record some of the promises God made to His chosen people of Israel, the Jews.

Genesis 12:2–3 (to Abraham)

_____

_____

_____

2 Samuel 7:22–24 (to David)

_____

_____

_____

3   In **Ephesians 2:11–13**, it says the Gentiles were without citizenship, promises, or hope, and without God. Read **Ephesians 2:13** where we see the glorious words "but God", which changes everything. Record what you learn in verse 13.

_____

_____

_____

4   What do the following verses say about our position after Jesus' death?

Our citizenship – Philippians 3:20–21:

_____

_____

_____

Our promises – Galatians 3:13–14:

_____

_____

_____

Our hope – 2 Thessalonians 2:16–17:

_____

_____

_____

Our relationship with God – Romans 8:13–15:

_____

_____

_____

5   Those who have come to know Jesus Christ as their personal Savior have a "but God" story. As non-Christians, they were on a path to destruction, but God intervened and changed their lives. What is your "but God" story? *If you are unsure if you know Jesus as your Savior, please see the box, "How to Know Jesus".*

_____

_____

_____

_____

_____

HOW TO KNOW JESUS

Sweet friend, there is no greater joy than being at peace with God and knowing that you will live in eternity with Him. Being a good person, going to church, or giving money to charities, for example, are all good things and come from a good heart. The problem is that by God's standard, good people don't go to heaven when they die. Only holy people go to heaven.

While that may sound impossible, it isn't. Every one of us has sin in our lives—things we have done that are displeasing to and disobedient to God. Whether we told a little white lie, committed a heinous crime, or did anything in between, it is all sin. And in God's eyes, the debt of sin must be paid.

And the payment for and the penalty for sin is death.

Jesus Christ was God's Son, born of a virgin. He lived a perfect and sinless life on earth for 33 years until He was crucified. Because He was a sinless, spotless sacrifice, His death paid the penalty for sin.

The question is, will you accept the death of Jesus in your place to pay the debt you owe God for your sin, or do you want to pay the debt on your own? One day, we will stand before God, and He will ask about our payment method. If you have accepted the gift of Jesus as your payment, you will enter into eternity with God. If you decided to reject Jesus and make the payment on your own by trying to be good enough to get in, God will require you to make the payment of your spiritual death for your sin—eternal separation from God in a place of torment. If you have waited until after you are face-to-face with God to call on the name of Jesus, you will be too late.

So how do you accept Jesus' death as payment for your sin now?

Simply pray the prayer below. *Prayer is simply talking with God silently or out loud.*

_____

DEAR GOD, I ADMIT THAT I HAVE SIN IN MY LIFE AND HAVE DONE THINGS THAT ARE DISPLEASING AND DISOBEDIENT TO YOU AND YOUR WORD. PLEASE FORGIVE ME OF MY SIN. I ACCEPT THE PAYMENT THAT YOUR SON, JESUS, MADE ON THE CROSS IN MY PLACE. I ACCEPT YOUR SON AS MY SAVIOR, SAVING ME FROM BEING ETERNALLY SEPARATED FROM YOU. JESUS, PLEASE COME INTO MY HEART. AMEN.

_____

Is it really that simple? Is it really just praying that simple prayer? Yes, it is! If you are truly sorry for your actions against God and accept the payment of Jesus to cover them, then through God's forgiveness and grace you are saved.

If you prayed this prayer, I encourage you to tell someone—a Christian friend, a pastor, a church leader, or someone else—and get connected with your local church so you can grow in your newfound salvation.

DAY 3
— READ *EPHESIANS 2:14-17* —

The cause of hostility between Jew and Gentile was the Law—a set of rules established by God to show humans it is impossible to live a perfect life. These laws were designed to show mankind their need for a Savior. God also gave David requirements regarding the building of the temple in Jerusalem. The temple was constructed with an area called the Holy of Holies as the centerpiece where the presence of God dwelled, and people were not permitted in His presence. One day a year, on the Day of Atonement, a priest was appointed to enter and offer a blood sacrifice at the altar of God to cover the sins of the Jewish nation and gain forgiveness for their transgressions.

To keep the sacred Holy of Holies protected, a thick, heavy veil (or drape) separated the area from the rest of the temple structure. Man's separation from God and requirement to fulfill the Law was in place for hundreds of years. But God sent His Son, Jesus, who lived a perfect life and fulfilled the Law in every way. He came against the religious leaders and invited the sinner into His presence, which made the Jewish leaders angry, especially when Jesus claimed to be the long-awaited Messiah. Their anger grew to the point of orchestrating the crucifixion of Jesus.

However, at Jesus' death, the veil in the temple that separated people from God was torn in two, and the separation was gone. Jesus was the fulfillment of the laws God had established. He lived a righteous, sinless life and paid the penalty of sin for you and me. He was the final, perfect sacrifice who did away with the need for any more sacrifices. Through faith and by trusting the sacrifice of Jesus to pay the penalty for our sin, we all (whether Jew or Gentile) stand righteous and holy before God. And we can finally be at peace with God.

1   Read **Ephesians 2:14**. Underline the word *peace* in your Bible. What does this verse say that Jesus has done?

_____

_____

_____

_____

2   In some versions of the Bible, **Ephesians 2:14** says that Jesus is our peace. Using a dictionary, look up the meaning of the word *peace*.

_____

_____

_____

_____

_____

_____

3   **Ephesians 2:11–22** speaks of the unity that Jesus' death and resurrection created. Read **Ephesians 2:15–17**. What do these verses say Jesus did for Jews and Gentiles?

The references to both in these verses is referring to two groups of people—
the Jews and the Gentiles.

_____

_____

_____

_____

_____

_____

4   It was God's plan from the beginning to include the Gentiles in His plan of salvation. Record what the following verses say about this.

Matthew 12:18–21

_____

_____

_____

Romans 3:27–30

_____

_____

_____

Romans 15:8–12

_____

_____

_____

5 How do you feel knowing that God has provided for your salvation? While this is a very familiar verse, look up **John 3:16** in several versions of the Bible, if possible. Record your favorite translation of **John 3:16** below, inserting your name and thanking God for what He did for you.

_____

_____

_____

_____

_____

DAY 4
— READ *EPHESIANS 2:18-22* —

It may be hard to imagine the hostility that existed between the Jews and the Gentiles in the early days of Christianity. We need to remember the viewpoint of the Jews of that day. They had been given the Promised Land, were called to be separated as God's chosen people and race, had received the promise of their coming Messiah, and knew of all God's promises of blessing and provision given to His chosen race—the Jews.

We also need to remember that the first converts to Christianity were mostly Jewish. Given their religious laws, especially concerning the separation of Jew and Gentile, it would be easy for them to continue thinking that Jehovah God, Jesus the Messiah, and the blessings and promises of faith in Him were only for the Jews. Can you imagine how difficult it was for them to understand that Gentiles were welcomed into God's family?

So Paul addresses the issue head-on. He clearly states there is no difference between Jew and Gentile since all things have come together as one in Christ. All who accept God's gift of grace will find peace with Him. Jesus brought peace between God and all sinners. His purpose has been and will always be to draw all people unto Himself and offer them salvation through faith in His Son Jesus Christ. It is His free gift of grace.

1   Paul has been writing about the unification of the Jews and the Gentiles in **Ephesians 2**. What does it say that both groups of people have through Jesus in **Ephesians 2:18**?

_____

_____

_____

Also in this verse, Paul mentions all three members of the Holy Trinity. What do you see as the work of Jesus, the Holy Spirit, and God the Father according to this verse?

_____

_____

_____

2   Because of the peace we have with God due to the work of Christ on the cross on our behalf, we are welcomed and invited into the presence of God.

How is that expressed in the following verses?

Matthew 11:28–29

_____

_____

_____

Romans 5:1–2

_____

_____

_____

Hebrews 4:15–16

_____

_____

_____

3   Read **Ephesians 2:19–21**. These verses tell us we are no longer strangers to God without a home.

- What does **verse 19** say we are instead?

_____

_____

_____

- What is the foundation of our household according to **Ephesians 2:20a**?

  _____

  _____

  _____

- In **Ephesians 2:20b**, who is the cornerstone?

  _____

  _____

  _____

- In Jesus, what does this household or structure do according to **Ephesians 2:21**?

  _____

  _____

  _____

4. What do you learn in **Ephesians 2:22** that furthers the thought from the previous verse?

  _____

  _____

  _____

5. It was God's plan from the beginning to include the Gentiles in His plan of salvation. Record what the following verses say about this.

John 14:16–17

  _____

  _____

  _____

1 Corinthians 3:16–17

  _____

  _____

  _____

Galatians 4:4–6

  _____

  _____

  _____

6 We all have circumstances, relationships, and situations that weigh heavily on our hearts. What is weighing on you today, or in what area of your life do you need to find peace? Write a prayer to Him below, boldly asking Him for what you need.

_____

_____

_____

_____

_____

_____

DAY 5
— READ *EPHESIANS 3:1-13* —

Paul's message was about the mystery of Christ that had been revealed. In this context, *mystery* is "a truth that was hidden by God in times past and is now revealed to those in His family." This is a "sacred secret," if you will, that is unknown by unbelievers but treasured by the people of God.

1 Read **Ephesians 3:1**. Paul wrote four of his epistles (or letters)—Ephesians, Philippians, Colossians, and Philemon—while he was in prison. What do you learn about Paul's suffering in **2 Corinthians 11:22–33**?

_____

_____

_____

2 Read **Ephesians 3:2–6**. What is the mystery Paul is speaking of (see **verse 6** specifically)?

_____

_____

_____

3 How does **Colossians 1:25–27** restate this mystery?

_____

_____

_____

_____

_____

_____

4 How does Paul describe himself in **Ephesians 3:7–12**?

_____

_____

_____

_____

_____

_____

5 Paul had an amazing perspective. He knew God had called him, and he was not afraid to live for Him, whatever the cost. We also have a calling, spiritual gifts, opportunities, skills, knowledge, and every other blessing given to us by the Lord. While we know that salvation is a gift of God's grace alone, we also have a responsibility once we are saved to do spiritual works. What do the following verses say about working for God.

1 Corinthians 15:58

_____

_____

_____

Colossians 3:23–24

_____

_____

_____

1 Thessalonians 1:2–3

_____

_____

_____

Concluding Thoughts

Lately, I have had restless thoughts. Life has thrown some difficult punches at me, so I'm tired and feel a bit defeated. My emotions are somewhat raw and running a bit wild, so I am the perfect target for Satan to throw some darts. Feelings of inadequacy, frustration, loneliness, bitterness, and hopelessness can seem like they are taking over, and it is so easy to forget all we are and all we have in Jesus.

I needed to be reminded this week that Paul had an amazing spiritual perspective and didn't let his circumstances define him. My goodness, he endured beatings, imprisonments, sufferings, and the like and never let them distract him or defeat him from accomplishing all God had given him to do.

We also need to have a good perspective on the circumstances of life. When the only thing we focus on is our immediate situation, our circumstances control us. We feel good when our circumstances are favorable but miserable when they are not. When our perspective is divine, we live with total trust in God's purposes because we know He knows our future and that every aspect of our lives is totally in God's hands.

Do not forget that Jesus is your peace, just as He is my peace. He is your way out of those repetitive, negative messages that play over and over in your head. He is your way out of depression. He is your way out of negativity. In Jesus there is peace, and that peace allows us to walk in freedom. That is the hope I cling to when my restless thoughts try to carry me away from the truth in Christ.

Jesus alone is our peace—there is no other source. Sin is the cause of all conflict and division; it is the enemy of peace and harmony. Peace comes only when our self-reliance and self-centeredness die. And the only place our selfishness truly dies is at the foot of the cross.

Are you willing to lay yourself down at the cross of Christ and allow His peace to flood through you? Are you willing to let Jesus, who is your peace, live in and through you?

Additional Notes

_____
_____
_____
_____
_____
_____
_____
_____
_____
_____
_____
_____
_____
_____
_____
_____
_____
_____
_____
_____
_____
_____
_____
_____
_____
_____
_____
_____
_____

LESSON THREE

Two Prayers

— EPHESIANS 1:15–23, 3:14–21 —

In the verses we will concentrate on this week, Paul states that he prays continually for the Ephesians, and he records two of those countless prayers in his letter to them. The first prayer, found in **Ephesians 1:15–23**, emphasizes the enlightenment of the Ephesians. The word enlighten generally means "to instruct or illuminate." This type of transforming enlightenment does not come from human instruction or book learning; instead, it must be given by the Holy Spirit. So Paul prays for the Ephesians to be given this instruction or illumination to fully understand what they have been given in Christ.

In the second prayer, found in **Ephesians 3:14–21**, Paul prays that the Ephesians will be empowered. That is the natural progression for someone who has first been enlightened. As the Ephesians grew to better understand the gifts God had given them, Paul prayed that they would make those gifts a vital part of their lives by faith. That is a beautiful prayer for strength to act in faith.

Paul's first prayer is for the readers of his letter to know God's power. His second prayer is for the readers to use that power. In those prayers, Paul expresses his desire for the Ephesians to know Jesus more, understand Him better, and live lives that correspond to the spiritual wealth they have in Christ.

Paul also encourages the Ephesians by commending their strong faith in God and the love they have for one another. Both of these attributes are indications of genuine salvation. I was immediately convicted by his words. I am so quick to give my friends a compliment about their new haircut or a stylish outfit, but how often do I let them know I admire their faith? How would you respond if a trusted friend told you they were encouraged by your faith or were challenged to read their Bible because of your command of Scripture? Let's not be afraid to tell others we are thankful for the ways they point us to Christ!

The second attribute Paul commends in the Ephesians is love. As Christians, we don't get to pick and choose who we get to love and who we can reject. Christ loves all believers, and so should we. To love like Christ is to love sacrificially and genuinely. It is defined as "an attitude of selfless sacrifice that results in generous acts of kindness done to others." **1 John 3:16–18** tells us to love not with word but in deed and action. When is the last time you did something for someone?

I remember several years ago when my mom was sick in the hospital. I had spent the entire day worrying about how I was going to get dinner together for my family, and I called home around 6:00 in the evening in a panic, trying to work out the details. My sweet daughter said, "Mom, don't worry about it. Mrs. Duncan just dropped off homemade spaghetti, salad, and garlic bread. We're eating now, and you can make a plate when you get home." I immediately hung up the phone to call my friend and could barely blubber thank you through my tears. Her response was this: "I'm really glad I listened to the Holy Spirit today. I felt that God was saying to make you a meal, so I did. In my head, it seemed like a bad idea, and I hadn't even talked to you about it. But my heart said to do it. I'm so glad I obeyed what the Spirit was saying to my heart." Love in deed! I wonder how many opportunities I have missed by rationalizing with my head and not obeying with my heart.

DAY 1
— READ *EPHESIANS 1:15-17* —

God deals with His children based on their future, not their past. While we so often see only our mistakes and shortcomings of the present, God sees exactly what we will be in all His fullness.

1   Read **Ephesians 1:15–17**. What are two things Paul had heard about the Ephesians? How often does Paul pray for the Ephesians? Who is blessed (or praised) in this verse?

_____

_____

_____

2   What specifically does Paul pray for them in **Ephesians 1:17**?

_____

_____

_____

3   What do you learn from the following verses about wisdom and knowledge?

Psalm 111:10

_____

_____

_____

Colossians 1:10–11

_____

_____

_____

James 3:17

_____

_____

_____

4

It is important to realize that Paul is praying for the Ephesians to receive spiritual wisdom and revelation. He does not want them to have more knowledge but rather to have the ability to understand all the magnificent blessings that were already theirs in Christ Jesus. This understanding comes from the Holy Spirit.

How do the following verses say that the Holy Spirit helps us?

John 14:26

_____

_____

_____

John 16:13

_____

_____

_____

1 Corinthians 2:11–12

_____

_____

_____

5

We can study God's Word, attend classes, and work at growing in knowledge; however, being able to apply that knowledge in godly wisdom comes from the Lord. **James 1:5** says that God will generously give wisdom to all who ask. Why not write a prayer to Him now, asking Him to give you wisdom?

_____

_____

_____

DAY 2
— READ *EPHESIANS 1:18* —

1   Read **Ephesians 1:18**, and record what Paul is asking the Lord for in this verse as he prays for the Ephesians.

_____

_____

_____

_____

_____

_____

_____

_____

2   According to the following verses, what is the hope we have in Jesus Christ?

Titus 2:13–14

_____

_____

_____

Titus 3:7

_____

_____

_____

1 Peter 1:3–4

_____

_____

_____

3   There are many things we can hope for in both the physical and spiritual realms. How do the following scriptures speak of hope?

Jeremiah 29:11

_____

_____

_____

Lamentations 3:22–24

_____

_____

_____

1 Peter 1:3–4

_____

_____

_____

4   In addition to hope, **Ephesians 1:18** also speaks of our glorious inheritance. Through salvation, God has adopted us as His own sons and daughters and allows us to share in the inheritance He promised His Son.

What do you learn from **Romans 8:14–18**?

_____

_____

_____

_____

5   Today we looked at our hearts, our hope, and the fact we are joint-heirs with Christ. Which of these areas challenged or encouraged you in your study?

_____

_____

_____

_____

_____

DAY 3
— READ *EPHESIANS 1:19–21* —

In yesterday's lesson, we looked at two areas in which Paul prayed the Ephesians would grow in knowledge: (1) that their hope, which lies in Jesus, would deepen, and (2) that they would further comprehend their glorious inheritance waiting in heaven. Today, we will look at their third area of enlightenment that Paul is asking God for growth.

1   What does Paul pray for his readers to be enlightened about in **Ephesians 1:19**?

_____

_____

_____

2   Read **Ephesians 1:20–21**, and record the phrases that speak of (a) the power of God and (b) the authority of Jesus Christ?

_____

_____

_____

"It is not enough to know God only as Saviour. We must get to know Him as Father, Friend, Guide, and the better we know Him, the more satisfying our spiritual lives will be."[6]

—*Warren Wiersbe*

3 Paul prays that the readers of his letter would come to know the immeasurable greatness of God's power seen in the resurrection of Christ. What do you learn about the power of the resurrection of Jesus from these verses?

Romans 1:3–4

_____

_____

_____

Romans 8:10–11

_____

_____

_____

4 Record what you learn about Jesus from **Philippians 2:5–11**.

_____

_____

_____

5 What thought or idea about the power of God or the resurrection and exaltation of Jesus has thrilled your soul today? Why not give God thanks for His marvelous works?

_____

_____

_____

DAY 4

— READ *EPHESIANS 3:14-19* —

In the second prayer, Paul prays that the readers of his letter would come to know God's power and walk in that power by faith. By nature, we are too weak to fully appreciate and appropriate the vast wealth we have in Christ or to use all His gifts for His glory in all their fullness. Jesus tells us in Matthew 26:41 that "the spirit indeed is willing, but the flesh is weak." We can try, but it is only through God's strength that we will succeed. It is God's power at work in us that enables us to use God's wealth.

Paul wants us to know the greatness of our spiritual power. That power is seen in His resurrection. He not only was raised from the dead but also ascended to heaven to sit down at the place of authority—at God's right hand. I love the mental picture of Christ being seated. It reminds me that His work on the cross for my salvation, justification, and glorification is finished. Hallelujah!

1

Paul makes four requests in His prayer to God in **Ephesians 3:14–19**. Write down each request

Look for the words "may" or "know" to help you find the requests.

Ephesians 3:16

_____

_____

_____

Ephesians 3:17

_____

_____

_____

Ephesians 3:18–19a

_____

_____

_____

Ephesians 3:19b

_____

_____

_____

2

How do the following verses say we are strengthened?

Isaiah 40:28–29

_____

_____

_____

Psalm 68:35

_____

_____

_____

3

Scripture tells us that upon salvation, the Holy Spirit comes to reside in our hearts. What do the verses below tell us regarding how we are saved?

Acts 3:19

_____

_____

_____

1 John 1:9

_____

_____

_____

Romans 10:9–10

_____

_____

_____

1 John 4:14–16

_____

_____

_____

4 God's love for you is immense. He loves you more than you can ever imagine and deeper than you can ever truly know. What do you learn of the love of God from the following verses?

Micah 7:18–19

_____

_____

_____

Zephaniah 3:17

_____

_____

_____

Romans 5:8

_____

_____

_____

Romans 8:38–39

_____

_____

_____

"It is through prayer that we lay hold of God's riches that enable us to behave like Christians and battle like Christians. Whether we actually bow our knees is not the important thing; that we bow our hearts and wills to the Lord and ask Him for what we need is the vital matter."[7]

—*Warren Wiersbe*

5 Reread **Romans 8:38–39**, and write the verse below, inserting your name.

_____

_____

_____

_____

_____

DAY 5
— READ EPHESIANS 3:20-21 —

1 Read **Ephesians 3:20–21 below**. What does this verse mean to you?

"Now to him who is able to do far more abundantly than all that we ask or think, according to the power at work within us, to him be glory in the church and in Christ Jesus throughout all generations, forever and ever. Amen."

_____

_____

_____

2 In the verse above, circle the words _"far more abundantly."_ What do you learn about the abundance of God from the following Psalms?

Psalm 31:19

_____

_____

_____

Psalm 69:13, 16

_____

_____

_____

Psalm 147:5

_____

_____

_____

3 Underline the phrase "power at work within us" in **Ephesians 3:20–21**.

What do you learn about the power of God from the verses below?

Exodus 15:6–7

_____

_____

_____

1 Chronicles 29:11–12

_____

_____

_____

2 Peter 1:3–4

_____

_____

_____

4 We have studied two beautiful prayers written by Paul for the Ephesians. Paul was confident in the power of God to answer his prayers and God's ability to answer in exceeding abundance. God has the power to answer your prayers too.

Reflecting on all you have studied, how are you encouraged by **John 15:7–8**?

_____

_____

_____

5 Sometimes we can feel inadequate bringing our prayers before the Lord. How does **Romans 8:26–27** encourage you about the provision of God and the depth that He cares for you?

_____

_____

_____

6 Reflect on all you have learned about God's abundance and power and prayer. What would you like to ask of Him today?

_____

_____

_____

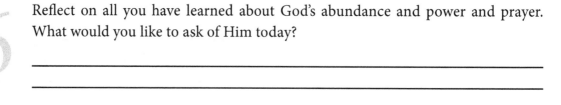

Concluding Thoughts

Paul recorded these two beautiful prayers for the Ephesians to be instructed and empowered by the Holy Spirit. Thankfully, the instruction of the Holy Spirit is imparted not only to the Ephesians in Paul's day but also to all believers. It is simply impossible to fully understand the things of God with our natural minds. We need the Holy Spirit to reveal the truth to us and then give us the power to put those truths into practice. And as with his first prayer, the applications are not only for those in Paul's day; they are needed for our lives as well.

In applying this prayer to the present, God's children not only need the enlightenment of their minds but also their hearts to gain a deeper understanding of God. Once we have gained a deeper knowledge of Him, we then need the strength and wisdom that comes from the Holy Spirit to not only hear God's Word but to put it into action in our daily lives.

The Bible tells us to pray continually and to pray about everything, but how much time do we really spend in prayer, and what do we spend our time praying about? Of course, we pray for our physical needs, our family, and our friends, but we need to remember that our spiritual nature needs prayer just as much as our physical nature. Unfortunately, I think too often we neglect the spiritual and give almost all of our attention to our physical needs.

We pray for food and a roof over our heads and our children's protection (and good grades); we pray for those who are sick and traveling; we pray for homes to sell and new jobs to be found. But how often do we pray for our spiritual well-being and the spiritual well-being of others around us? How often do we pray for God's peace in our troubled souls, for contentment with God's love alone, or for us to know Him more and love Him more deeply?

Can you even begin to imagine the source of power, strength, love, and grace that is at your disposal if you prayed for God to meet your spiritual needs and not just your physical needs? All this is available to us if we are willing to give up the right to control our lives and circumstances and allow ourselves to be completely yielded to Him.

When we truly understand all the blessings God has given us, we should be willing to completely surrender to Him—to give ourselves fully to be used by Him. Just think what He could do in and through you if you asked Him to take complete control of your life. He has the power to give superabundantly more than we can ask or imagine. Are you willing to give Him all and unleash His unlimited power in your life?

Oh, friend, may that be your prayer!

Additional Notes

_____
_____
_____
_____
_____
_____
_____
_____
_____
_____
_____
_____
_____
_____
_____
_____
_____
_____

LESSON FOUR

Unity

— EPHESIANS 4:1–16 —

The first three chapters of Ephesians have recorded the blessing of our riches in Jesus Christ. Now in the last three chapters, we will look at our responsibilities in Christ. This is not like God's conditional blessing in the Old Testament of "if you obey Me, I will bless you." This is a New Testament command—"because I have already blessed you, now, in response to My love and My grace, obey Me."

It is always interesting to me how many people want the blessing of God and want Him to answer their prayers but are reluctant or even defiant when they are asked to obey what God's Word says. John MacArthur said, "Too many Christians are glad to have the spiritual security, blessings, and promises of the gospel but have too little sense of responsibility in conforming to its standards and obeying its commands."[8]

I'm not going to tell you that the coming weeks will be an easy study because, at times, the Word of God may challenge you in new ways and may even seem to be demanding. We will hear God's instruction, and it may convict our thinking or ways we are out of the will of God. We will want to find ways to excuse our behavior and lack of obedience.

If you find that His Word is piercing your heart, be quick to repent and look for ways to deepen your walk with Jesus by growing in maturity in your relationship with Him. I think that may be why Paul put such an exhaustive list of blessings at the beginning of the book—to remind us how grateful we need to be and how quickly we should bow our knees to anything God asks us to do.

To turn the corner, Paul begins with a little transitional word, "therefore," marking the transition from positional to practical truth, from doctrine to duty, and from principle to practice. As we move into this section of teaching, Paul is saying, "In view of all God has done, walk worthy!"

This week, we are going to look at how to have unity in the body of Christ and how God has given us all spiritual gifts to be used for ministry and building one another up in Christ.

DAY 1
— READ *EPHESIANS 4:1-3* —

1

Read **Ephesians 4:1–3**. In verse 1, we see the call to "walk worthy." How does Paul describe that walk, in verses 2 and 3?

_____

_____

_____

_____

_____

_____

2

As we saw in **Ephesians 4:2**, Paul first tells us that a worthy walk is marked with humility and gentleness. As we look into a better understanding of humility, it is helpful to also study the opposite of humility, which is pride.

What do you learn about pride and humility in the following verses?

Proverbs 11:2

_____

_____

_____

Philippians 2:3–4

_____

_____

_____

1 Peter 5:5–7

_____

_____

_____

Christ is the standard by which we can measure righteousness. He is holy. How am I measuring up? He is righteous. How am I doing? He showed love and grace to all. Am I even close? Chances are, we fall miserably short, and when we see how badly we miss the mark, it should drive us to repentance. John MacArthur said, "Our business success, fame, education, wealth, personality, good works or anything else we are or have in ourselves counts for nothing before God. The more we rely on and glory in such things, the greater barrier they become in our communion with God. Every person comes before the Lord with nothing to commend him and everything to condemn him. But when he comes with the spirit of the penitent tax-collector, saying 'God be merciful to me, the sinner,' God will willingly and lovingly accept him."[9] That is an attitude of humility. It says Christ first, others second, and self last.

3 Humility always produces gentleness, which is defined as power under the control of God. A gentle person responds willingly to the Word of God, no matter what the requirements or consequences. What do you learn about gentleness or meekness from the following verses?

Isaiah 29:19

_____

_____

_____

Titus 3:1–2

_____

_____

_____

James 3:13–14

_____

_____

_____

4 Another characteristic that should be evidenced in our walk with Christ is patience. How do the following verses aid in your understanding of being patient?

Romans 12:12

_____

_____

_____

1 Thessalonians 5:14–15

_____

_____

_____

5 If we are going to strive for unity in our relationships, we must love our neighbors as ourselves. **First Corinthians 13** is one of the greatest passages on love in the Bible. Read **1 Corinthians 13:1–7**, and record the characteristics of love that are listed in the passage.

_____

_____

_____

_____

_____

_____

DAY 2
— READ *EPHESIANS 4:4–7* —

1 Read **Ephesians 4:4–7**, and circle the word "one" in your Bible. How often does the word one appear in these verses?

_____

_____

_____

2

These verses reference the complete Trinity—God the Father, Jesus the Son, and the Holy Spirit. Which members of the Trinity are referenced in the verses below?

Ephesians 4:4

_____

_____

_____

Ephesians 4:5

_____

_____

_____

Ephesians 4:6

_____

_____

_____

3

John 17:20–23 records Jesus' prayer in the Upper Room before His crucifixion. What do you learn about Jesus' desire for His followers to be unified?

_____

_____

_____

_____

_____

_____

4

What do the following verses say about unity?

Psalm 133:1

_____

_____

_____

Romans 12:3–5

_____

_____

_____

1 Peter 3:8

_____

_____

_____

5 What does **Matthew 5:22–24** say about being reconciled with your brothers and sisters in Christ? As you think about these verses and our lesson on unity today, is there a broken relationship that God may be asking you to work on repairing? What steps will you take to move toward reconciliation?

_____

_____

_____

_____

_____

_____

THEREFORE IT SAYS, "WHEN HE ASCENDED ON HIGH HE LED A HOST OF CAPTIVES, AND HE GAVE GIFTS TO MEN." (IN SAYING, "HE ASCENDED," WHAT DOES IT MEAN BUT THAT HE HAD ALSO DESCENDED INTO THE LOWER REGIONS, THE EARTH? HE WHO DESCENDED IS THE ONE WHO ALSO ASCENDED FAR ABOVE ALL THE HEAVENS, THAT HE MIGHT FILL ALL THINGS.)

—Ephesians 4:8-10

As we study Scripture, sometimes we read passages that seem to be confusing, and possibly this one seems difficult when you read it. I think we can all agree that Jesus was in heaven with God and descended to earth to live life in human form, was crucified, buried, and resurrected, and then ascended back to heaven following His resurrection. But many people do not know that following His death and before His resurrection, Jesus also descended to what we refer to as hell.

If we look back in the Old Testament, the writers refer 66 times to a place for the dead called Sheol. Sheol was located in the center of the earth and was the place all souls went upon death whether they had been faithful to God or not. Sheol was separated from the presence of God because the penalty for the sins of the people had not yet been paid by Jesus' death on the cross.

Remember, God made it clear from the first sin of Adam and Eve that the penalty of sin was death and that only through the blood sacrifice of a perfect Lamb would there be forgiveness of sin. God also promised that one day He would send a Messiah, a Savior, for the sinful, to be the once and for all perfect Lamb who would be sacrificed for their sins, paying the penalty for sin for all.

Before Jesus came to earth, those who believed by faith that God would send the Messiah and recognized their need for a Savior, God counted their faith in the coming Messiah as faithfulness to His call. They recognized their sin and their need for a Redeemer who only God could provide. Those who did not recognize their need were counted as rejecting God and His Messiah.

Sheol was a place where the faithful were waiting for the promised Messiah to redeem them. From **Luke 16:19–28**, we see there are two sections in Sheol—Abraham's Bosom (also called Abraham's Side) and hell (a place of torment). The faithful were waiting for the Redeemer in Abraham's bosom, and the unfaithful were in torment in hell.

At Jesus' death, where did He go for the three days He was in the grave? I believe He went to Sheol. **1 Peter 3:19** says that Jesus preached to the spirits in prison and references mankind. After His death and before His resurrection, the only place where mankind's spirits were at this point in history was Sheol. We also know that Jesus was not in heaven because He told Mary Magdalene when she saw Him in the garden following His resurrection that He had not yet ascended to His Father.

After Jesus' resurrection, Jesus went down to Sheol to redeem those in Abraham's bosom and also to proclaim that He was the Messiah to those who were in hell. Three days after His crucifixion, He rose to life again and spent 40 days on earth before returning to His Father's side in heaven. Today, He is seated at God's right hand in victory and authority.

DAY 3
— READ *EPHESIANS 4:11-12* —

Unity should be the concern of every believer, and we need to consistently work toward harmony in our relationships with others and unity within the church. But we also need to remember that unity is not uniformity—we're not going to all look alike. Yes, God wants us as His children to be unified as one, but He has also created us to be unique.

Part of our unique gifting is how God equips us for service by giving us spiritual gifts. God gives these gifts to us at the time of our salvation to be used for the common good of the church. They are not talents, skills, or abilities; nonbelievers can have all these things. Salvation is required to receive spiritual gifts.

1   Read **Ephesians 4:11–12**. What are the categories of ministry "jobs" listed in these verses?

_____

_____

_____

2   There are two other passages in the Bible where spiritual gifts are listed. Compare these two passages by making a list of the gifts listed in each one.

1 CORINTHIANS 12:8-11, 28   **ROMANS 12:4-8**

3 Looking back at **1 Corinthians 12**, what do you learn in verses 4–7? What do you see as the purpose of spiritual gifts **(verse 7)**?

_____

_____

_____

4 What result do you see in the following verses that can happen when we are unified and use our gifts to build up others and encourage believers?

Matthew 5:15–16

_____

_____

_____

Romans 15:5–6

_____

_____

_____

1 Corinthians 10:32–33

_____

_____

_____

2 Corinthians 9:7, 12–13

_____

_____

_____

5 Every believer in Jesus Christ has been given at least one spiritual gift, if not more. Why not write a prayer to God, asking Him to show you how you can use your spiritual gifts for His kingdom? If you do not know your spiritual gift, write a prayer asking God to help you identify how He has gifted you.

_____

_____

_____

_____

DAY 4
— READ *EPHESIANS 4:13-14* —

Yesterday in our study we looked at spiritual gifting and the purpose of those gifts—to equip the individual for ministry and build up the body of Christ. Today we will look more deeply into the purpose of these gifts.

1 According to **Ephesians 4:13**, how long will we use our spiritual gifts?

_____

_____

_____

2 How does **Ephesians 4:14** describe the nature of children?

_____

_____

_____

3 While God's desire is for us is to mature in our faith and grow in our relationship with Him, I have always loved that He consistently calls us His children. He understands that we are not always going to have things together, that we are going to act immaturely at times, and that we have a great need for a Father. Yet He invites us to call Him Abba, or Daddy and allows us to crawl in His lap to pour out our hearts before Him (**Psalm 62:8**). Read **Matthew 19:13–14**. Although it is speaking of earthly children, I believe it shows Jesus' attitude in welcoming all of us into His presence.

How does this thought encourage you today?

_____

_____

_____

_____

_____

4 What are some ways we can grow in our faith and mature in our relationship with Jesus?

Hebrews 10:23–25

_____
_____
_____

2 Peter 3:17–18

_____
_____
_____

5 Read **Colossians 1:9–14**, and write the prayer in the verses below, inserting your name where appropriate.

_____
_____
_____
_____
_____
_____

DAY 5
— READ *EPHESIANS 4:15-16* —

1 What does **Ephesians 4:15a** say about our speech?

_____
_____
_____
_____

2 There are times when we feel we should speak with a friend or a loved one about difficult things, such as when they are walking in sin or disobedience. First, we must pray for God's wisdom and ensure He is asking us to speak to our friend. Once we are certain of God's leading, we should go to our friend in love. According to **2 Timothy 3:16–17**, what should be the basis of our conversation?

_____

_____

_____

3 How do the following verses add to your understanding of the words that come from our mouths?

Psalm 19:14

_____

_____

_____

Proverbs 16:23–24

_____

_____

_____

Colossians 4:5–6

_____

_____

_____

4 Read **Ephesians 4:15b–16.** What do these verses say about Jesus Christ, and what do they say is the result or goal of being in Christ and walking in a worthy manner and using our spiritual gifts?

*The end of **verse 16** sums up the purpose of all 16 verses
we have been studying this week.*

_____

_____

_____

_____

_____

5 What do you learn about Jesus in **Colossians 1:15–20?**

_____

_____

_____

6 Read **Jude 1:24–25.** These verses are a beautiful benediction for our study this week. Write the verses below, inserting your name to claim personally what Jesus does for you and the authority He has over all?

_____

_____

_____

_____

_____

_____

_____

Concluding Thoughts

The word *worthy* means "having adequate merit, character, or value." Basically, we are to walk on a level commensurate with the position we have in Christ—a position of holiness and righteousness, of being God's child. So, the question is, do I walk in a manner that has adequate merit, character, or value considering that I am holy and a child of God? Do you walk in that manner?

The word *walk* is used many times in the New Testament and refers to a person's daily living. In Greek, the word *worthy* has the root meaning of "balancing the scales." That means our daily living should correspond to our high position as a child of God and fellow heir with Jesus. Our daily living is on one side of the scale, balancing our position in Him on the other. I dare to say that often my daily living falls far short of my position in Christ as His joint-heir.

If all Christians were walking in obedience to and in the power of the Holy Spirit, our doctrine and relationships would be purified and unified, and spiritual unity would result in complete harmony among God's people. But in all practicality, I don't know how often I even make it through the day walking worthy of my calling!

I see this list of ideals and realize how far I am from really bending my knee in submission to Him in all things, in all moments, and all ways. Guess what? God knows that! He knows that you and I are going to falter and fall, and He knows we are going to make mistakes. That's why I am so grateful that God calls us His *children*! At times, children struggle with obedience. They get selfish and whiny, and they fall down. But they are also quick to forgive and forget and quick to hop back up on their feet again, eager to please their daddy!

Oh, friend, it is all right to be human. At times, your feet will walk in a different direction than God's best. Your attitudes and actions will look more worldly and less godly. When this happens, simply return your attention to God, and surrender to His will for your life again. Ask Him to fill you with His strength, and submit to Him again. That will allow His Spirit to shine through you.

As you walk with God, He can bless others through you, knowing that your weakness and woundedness are the ways His glory can shine through you. God's strength and power show themselves most effectively in our weakness.

So, when you realize your actions and attitudes are not worthy of all the blessings and gifts God has lavished upon you, look up, ask for His forgiveness, and pray for His strength to keep walking. And remember, your actions and good works don't make you worthy—Jesus does.

Hallelujah!

Additional Notes

_____
_____
_____
_____
_____
_____
_____
_____
_____
_____

LESSON FIVE

Practical Living

— EPHESIANS 4:17-29 —

Last week we looked at the idea of walking worthy of our calling in Jesus Christ and remembering all the blessings we have received in Christ. This week we will see Paul giving the Ephesians practical ways to walk and live every day. He understood the battle of our will and expressed his own personal struggle in Romans.

> **FOR I DO NOT UNDERSTAND MY OWN ACTIONS. FOR I DO NOT DO WHAT I WANT, BUT I DO THE VERY THING I HATE. NOW IF I DO WHAT I DO NOT WANT, I AGREE WITH THE LAW, THAT IT IS GOOD. SO NOW IT IS NO LONGER I WHO DO IT, BUT SIN THAT DWELLS WITHIN ME. FOR I KNOW THAT NOTHING GOOD DWELLS IN ME, THAT IS, IN MY FLESH. FOR I HAVE THE DESIRE TO DO WHAT IS RIGHT, BUT NOT THE ABILITY TO CARRY IT OUT. FOR I DO NOT DO THE GOOD I WANT, BUT THE EVIL I DO NOT WANT IS WHAT I KEEP ON DOING. NOW IF I DO WHAT I DO NOT WANT, IT IS NO LONGER I WHO DO IT, BUT SIN THAT DWELLS WITHIN ME.**

> *—Romans 7:15–20*

Goodness! I feel like I could have written that statement because I struggle all the time with wanting to honor God in everything I do, yet I keep finding myself in sin. How about you? Do you feel the same struggle? That battle is between the old self—who we were before we met Jesus—and the new self—the new creature we have become in Jesus. Saving faith in Jesus doesn't just add something to our nature. We don't simply receive something new; God makes us something new altogether! We are a new creation! Our old nature dies, and we are completely transformed!

Unfortunately, even though we have this new nature that is holy and righteous, we continue to sin after we come to salvation through Jesus. Yes, our old nature has been crucified, but our desire for sin remains in our flesh. We are tempted, and we are weak, so we will sin. Until the day we are living with Jesus in heaven, we will be limited by our flesh. That means our new nature will be limited as we live and serve others. One day in heaven we will be complete in Him. Until then, our imperfections will sometimes be seen in our flesh, even as we try to walk worthily.

It is important to note that Scripture does not say we have two natures. We have only one—the new nature we have received in Christ. The old nature has been crucified with Christ, and only the new nature now lives in us. God has transformed our hearts and our souls. We are made new on the inside. And while there is not a remaining old nature, there is the remaining exterior of sinful flesh that causes Christians to sin. So, while believers are transformed on the inside, they are not perfect in their thoughts and actions. We are not completely perfect until we are united with Christ in heaven at death. So, while we still may have a desire to sin, that desire no longer has authority over us! That is an important distinction.

As we lay aside our flesh and allow our new selves to be controlled by God, our actions and behavior will evidence the change God has brought about in our lives. Every moment we need to choose to die to our flesh and walk in our new nature.

As Paul gives us the characteristics of those who are ungodly, it is important to understand that he is referring to those who live in habitual sin and have an ungodly lifestyle. It is their mindset to walk in the ways opposite to God because they do not know Him. Since they have not recognized their need for Him, their life does not reflect Him. Instead . . .

1. Their minds are futile. The word futile means "without purpose or pointless." Those of a futile mind have no reason to live in a way that pleases God, and they find satisfaction in sinful things and actions, even going so far as to rationalize their lifestyle.

2. They are darkened in their understanding, not knowing or understanding the things of God or moral values. There is a hardness in their hearts toward God, and they are unresponsive to the truths found in His Word.

3. They are calloused. They are apathetic and insensitive about the ways of God and godliness. They do not care about the consequences of their thoughts or actions.

4. They are given to sin and live solely by their own desires. Because they do not have a reason to restrain their actions, they live an ungodly lifestyle and ignore any guilt that might tell them to act otherwise.

As God's children, we are different. We are not the ungodly but rather the saved! We have a different way of life and a different way of thinking. Remember, we are new! So, our new walk in Christ is the exact opposite of the ungodly. Our walk is Christ-centered and purposeful. It knows and understands the truths of God's Word, and it is sensitive to sin. That is our new self.

DAY 1
— READ *EPHESIANS 4:17–19* —

The word *Gentile* in this passage can refer to anyone who is not of Jewish descent, but it can also refer to anyone who does not know God or is a pagan. In addition, we can also have the characteristic of acting in an ungodly manner. A person who does not know God will be ungodly both in nature and in action. For those of us in Christ, our nature is made new and converted from pagan to Christian; however, until our will is fully submitted to the Holy Spirit, our actions can look more like those of the ungodly rather than the godly.

In the verses today, we will look at the actions of the ungodly (sometimes called Gentiles or pagans) and Paul's charge to those in Christ to be careful to walk worthy and not as the ungodly. Today's verses might be a struggle to get through but just wait. Tomorrow we will turn a corner and see what God can do through Jesus! Also, remember that every one of us was at one time pagans and in need of a Savior. While we were sinners, Christ died for you and me . . . and for the entire world.

1   Read **Ephesians 4:17**. What is Paul's instruction in this verse?

_____

_____

_____

2   According to **Ephesians 4:18–19**, how do the Gentiles (those who do not know God) live?

_____

_____

_____

_____

_____

_____

_____

3 What do you learn from the following verses about God and His love for the ungodly?

Romans 5:6–8

_____

_____

_____

Colossians 1:26–27

_____

_____

_____

2 Peter 3:9

_____

_____

_____

4 There is a hardness of heart with the ungodly, and because of that, they are unresponsive to truth.

What do you learn further from the following scripture references?

Proverbs 28:13–14

_____

_____

_____

_____

Zechariah 7:11–13

_____

_____

_____

_____

Romans 2:5

_____

_____

_____

_____

> "Fallen people pride themselves in their ability to reason. We consider this the highest function of humanity and take great pride in the human ability to ferret out knowledge and to put various items together to produce practical gadgets. We point with pride to the technological perfection of our modern developments, to the skill with which science has harnessed the forces of nature and made them servants of humanity. Humans exalt their reason, but in the eyes of God, human reasoning is empty and vain."[10]
>
> —*Ray Stedman*

5 The ungodly will also be apathetic and insensitive about moral and spiritual things. They will reject God's standards of righteousness and not care about the consequences of their thoughts and actions. How do these verses state this fact?

Mark 7:21–23

_____

_____

_____

Galatians 5:19–21

_____

_____

_____

Colossians 3:5–6

_____

_____

_____

6 It can be difficult to look at the sin of mankind, and we have spent the day doing just that! Tomorrow we will turn the corner with those glorious words "but you." Until then, read **Psalm 51:1–12**, and remember that even the vilest sin can be washed clean by the crimson blood of Jesus Christ.

Below, write the phrases from the Psalm that are particularly meaningful to you.

_____

_____

_____

_____

_____

_____

DAY 2
— READ *EPHESIANS 4:20-24* —

I have mentioned before that I love to see the word 'but' in Scripture. It reminds me of what I once was, but God has intervened and done something marvelous and wonderful in me and for me. As God's children, we are different. We are not the ungodly but the saved! We have a different way of life and a different way of thinking. Remember, we are new! So our new walk in Christ is the exact opposite of the ungodly. Our walk is Christ-centered and purposeful. It knows and understands the truth of God's Word, and it is sensitive to sin. This is our new self.

In our new nature, we possess the fullness of the divine nature. One day when we are face to face with Jesus, we will finally experience this new nature without the corruption of our unredeemed flesh. And we will finally be free.

1

Read **Ephesians 4:20–21.** What do you learn about Jesus from these verses?

_____

_____

_____

_____

_____

_____

> "Christianity is not merely a change in outward actions or a bit higher moral or ethical level. Christianity is a revolutionary change of government that results in a radical change in behavior."[11]
>
> —*Ray Stedman*

2   What do you learn about truth from the following verses from the Gospel of John?

John 1:17

_____

_____

_____

John 8:31–32

_____

_____

_____

John 14:6

_____

_____

_____

3   What are we to put *off* according to **Ephesians 4:22**?

_____

_____

_____

What are we to put *on* according to E**phesians 4:24**?

_____

_____

_____

4 How does **Ephesians 4:23** say we are to be renewed?

_____

_____

_____

5 How do the following verses state this concept?

Romans 12:1–2

_____

_____

_____

Colossians 3:9–10

_____

_____

_____

6 What does **Colossians 3:12–17** say we should put on as new creations in Jesus?

_____

_____

_____

"I have been crucified with Christ. It is no longer I who live, but Christ who lives in me. And the life I now live in the flesh I live by faith in the Son of God, who loved me and gave himself for me."

—Galatians 2:20

DAY 3
— READ *EPHESIANS 4:25–27* —

"The only reliable evidence of a person's being saved is not a past experience of receiving Christ, but a present life that reflects Christ. . . . New creatures act like new creatures."[12]

—John MacArthur

1   Read **Ephesians 4:25.** What are we to put away? How are we to speak to one another?

_____

_____

_____

2   **Luke 10:27–37** records the story of the Good Samaritan. What do you learn about who your neighbor is according to these verses?

_____

_____

_____

3   What does **Ephesians 4:26–27** instruct us to do?

_____

_____

_____

4   What do you learn about anger from the following verses?

Psalm 37:8

_____

_____

_____

Proverbs 14:29–30

_____

_____

_____

Proverbs 19:11

_____

_____

_____

Proverbs 29:22

_____

_____

_____

5 In contrast, God's anger is not sinful but is directed toward sin. His love for the sinner, however, is constant. What do you learn about God's anger from the verses below?

Psalm 86:15

_____

_____

_____

Psalm 103:8–9

_____

_____

_____

Joel 2:12–13

_____

_____

_____

Micah 7:18

_____

_____

_____

_____

6 As you considered what we have learned about anger and recall the story of the Good Samaritan, who might God be calling you to show mercy to this week? Write a prayer that asks God to allow you to minister to them this week. You may also have felt conviction over anger you have been holding onto in a relationship or situation you are facing, either currently or in the past. If so, ask God to forgive you of the sin of anger and give you the strength to act in mercy.

_____

_____

_____

_____

_____

_____

DAY 4
— READ *EPHESIANS 4:28* —

The verse we will look at today refers to the behavior of a thief. And while the idea of not stealing is pretty self-explanatory, for our study and reflection today, I want to consider the idea of "good labor," not only in the sense of working hard at our job or task but in working productively in an honorable job. As we work through Scripture today, are there compromises you are making in your job or task? Do you text friends or scroll through social media when you are being paid to work? Dare I ask how you are regarding your service to God? Are you stealing from Him by robbing Him of your time or talents? We may not be burglars, but at times, most of us (if not all of us) are guilty of stealing.

1 According to **Ephesians 4:28**, what is the thief not to do? What is the thief to do, and what is the reason for doing it?

_____

_____

_____

2   What do you learn from **Proverbs 16:2–3** about involving God in your work?

_____

_____

_____

3   In the verses below, what encouragement do you find to keep on working for the Lord?

1 Corinthians 15:58

_____

_____

_____

Hebrews 6:10–12

_____

_____

_____

4   According to **Colossians 3:23–24**, what is our motivation for working hard?

_____

_____

_____

What are we warned about in **2 Thessalonians 3:11–13**?

_____

_____

_____

5   Whether we are a student, a stay-at-home mom, a church volunteer, or a CEO of a major company, we all have jobs to do. For those of us who know Jesus as our Savior, our first responsibility is working for God's kingdom and bringing Him glory in all we do. In what ways in your work or service do you want to put Him first and serve Him better?

_____

_____

_____

_____

_____

DAY 5

— READ *EPHESIANS 4:29* —

Our focus verse today concerns our speech, which sometimes can be the hardest for us to control. Our words truly have the power to destroy another. Sometimes we use them to deliberately wound another person, and sometimes we carelessly throw them about as we gossip about others. Other times, we choose to withhold words of encouragement, blessing, or acceptance from someone who needs to hear our words. Our words can break hearts and ruin reputations. With a weapon that powerful, our tongue must be under the control of Jesus Christ at all times.

"God, please place Your arm around my shoulder and Your hand over my mouth."

—Unknown

1   What does **Ephesians 4:29** say concerning our speech?

_____

_____

_____

_____

_____

2   How do the following verses add to your understanding?

Proverbs 4:24

_____

_____

_____

Ephesians 5:4

_____

_____

_____

Colossians 3:8–9

_____

_____

_____

3

Scripture also warns us to be careful of others' words. What warning do you see in the following?

Proverbs 10:18–19

_____

_____

_____

Romans 16:17–18

_____

_____

_____

4

In **Matthew 12:33–37**, Jesus addresses careless words. What do you learn from His words?

_____

_____

_____

5

James 3:3–12 speaks of taming the tongue. Read through this passage, and write what you've learned below.

_____

_____

_____

_____

_____

6 Each one of us has wounded another person with a carelessly uttered word. Some days it seems like the filter for our words is on vacation. Anger, jealousy, or bitterness takes hold of our emotions, and words fly out of our mouths like arrows from a bow. 1 John 1:9 tells us that if we confess our sin, God is faithful and just to forgive us. Write a prayer to God below, asking Him to forgive your wounding words and to set a guard over your mouth.

Don't forget to celebrate His forgiveness!

_____

_____

_____

Concluding Thoughts

Romans 12:2 tells us to not be conformed to this world but to be transformed by the renewal of our minds that by testing we may discern what is the will of God, what is good and acceptable and perfect. I truly believe that if we could ever wrap our minds around our amazing, giving, loving God, our actions would be completely different.

Instead, we often take God and His great gifts for granted. Let me ask you this: What do you put in your mind? What do you watch on TV or listen to on the radio? Is it Bible-based, or is it based in the world? I don't know who said this, but it applies here.

What you do with your mind will determine a great deal of what you will become as a Christian. If you fill your mind only with the products of our secular culture, you will remain secular and sinful. On the other hand, if you feed it with the Bible and train toward godly conversation, and obey and apply biblical truths, you will grow in godliness. The Christian life is not just about modifying our behavior but changing our thinking. God doesn't make us nice; He makes us new.

—Source Unknown

So, our "job," if you will, is to completely surrender our entire life to Jesus because it is in combining our new nature with a new mindset that we will see God truly at work in our lives in incredible ways. Does it sound like I'm saying the same thing over and over again? Surrender is the key to the abundant Christian life, but it requires work and effort. Remember, your mind has control over every one of your actions.

Until you renew and change your mind, the world and your flesh are still going to control you because your mind is being so greatly influenced by the flesh and by the world. You have to be willing every moment to surrender your entire life to Jesus Christ and give Him complete control over your body, heart, soul, and mind.

We have the help of the Holy Spirit within us, but we must keep the lines of communication open by having a prayerful conversation with God all day long. Constantly listen for Jesus and the Holy Spirit to speak to your heart, your mind, your conscience, your sense of moral righteousness, your fairness, and your sense of what is right and godly. You cannot take your eyes off of Jesus for a second.

Having a renewed mind is difficult. It takes work, humility, and surrender, but the joy of walking that closely with Jesus moment by moment is an amazing journey.

Additional Notes

_____
_____
_____
_____
_____
_____
_____
_____
_____
_____
_____
_____
_____

LESSON SIX

Walking In Purity

— EPHESIANS 4:30–5:21 —

Paul has been challenging the Ephesians who are in Christ to walk worthy of their calling as holy children of God, richly blessed with a glorious inheritance. We have already seen that our walk should be characterized by humility, gentleness, patience, forbearing love, and unity. In addition, we should use our spiritual gifts for the good and encouragement of the body of Christ and lay aside our old, fleshly selves who love to linger in sinful habits. After all, that old self has been crucified with Christ and is dead! Paul told his readers to put on the new self—a beautiful new creation—who is controlled by and surrendered to the Spirit of God and to put away lying, stealing, and unwholesome talk.

Paul then sternly tells the Ephesians to not grieve the Holy Spirit (**Ephesians 4:30**). As we begin our study on this section, we need to understand what it means to grieve the Holy Spirit. The word grieve means to distress or cause great sorrow. Very simply, grieving the Holy Spirit is causing Him distress or great sorrow. And what causes that pain in Him? Our sin does. It breaks His heart!

Sin has consequences. First and foremost, it breaks your fellowship with God. It's like a wall you build that puts God on one side and you on the other. It's pretty hard to have a relationship when there is a wall between you and God. And the Holy Spirit is grieved because your fellowship with God has been broken. He knows the blessing you are missing; He knows the consequences of the sin you are holding onto with a stubborn hand, and He longs for the fellowship and relationship with God to be completely restored. He is distressed when you forfeit the joy and peace found in abiding in Christ to instead live in the fleeting pleasure of sin. His heart aches because your sin and my sin grieve Him.

And yet while we can grieve Him, we cannot do anything to make Him leave us. We are sealed! What an amazing thought! We have been sealed until the day of redemption when He will present us to Jesus. What a glorious thought! Paul wants us to be eternally grateful to the Holy Spirit for His making salvation impossible for us to lose and to see the tragedy of our refusal to put off our old natures when we find ourselves in sin.

Paul also wants us to recognize that we are to imitate God in the way we live and relate to others. In our study this week, Paul is calling his readers to walk in purity. It is a hard calling that could at times require lots of prayer and sacrifice. Remember, we are not saved and made good; we are made holy. Paul's instruction is that our actions reflect the holiness of God, displaying His love and grace to everyone.

"Despite all the works of God that are evident around us, both in the natural world and in the world of thought and ideas, there are really only two things that God ever does in human history: God creates and He redeems. Those are the two things. Everything in the whole universe gathers about these two. God creates and God redeems. God makes things live, and God heals that which is broken. It is because God is life and God is love. He is therefore our Maker and our Healer."[13]

—*Ray Stedman*

DAY 1
— READ *EPHESIANS 4:31-5:2* —

1 Read **Ephesians 4:31.** In a dictionary, look up the definitions of the following words:

Bitterness

_____

_____

_____

Wrath

_____

_____

_____

Anger

_____

_____

Clamor

_____

_____

Slander

_____

_____

Malice

_____

_____

_____

2

In contrast, read **Ephesians 4:32**, and then look up the definitions of these words:

Kind

_____

_____

Tenderhearted

_____

_____

Forgiving

_____

_____

_____

3   **Ephesians 4:32** instructs us to forgive one another just as we have been forgiven by God. His love and His grace toward us are our motivation for showing love and grace toward others. How does God show His forgiveness toward us according to **Colossians 2:13–14**?

_____

_____

_____

_____

_____

_____

4   Similarly, **Ephesians 5:1–2** tells us to imitate God and walk in love that He exemplified for us. What do the following verses say about this love?

John 3:16

_____

_____

_____

Galatians 2:20

_____

_____

_____

2 Thessalonians 2:16

_____

_____

_____

5   Read **1 John 4:7–11**. Insert your name in these verses, and write a prayer below asking God to help you grow to love others more and more.

_____

_____

_____

_____

_____

"Because our heavenly Father is holy, we are to be holy. Because He is kind, we are to be kind. Because He is forgiving, we are to be forgiving. Because God in Christ humbled Himself, we are to humble ourselves. Because God is love, as His beloved children, we are to walk in love. . . . The greatest evidence of love is undeserved forgiveness. . . . It is the supreme evidence of God's love, and the most convincing proof of our love."[14]

—John MacArthur

DAY 2
— READ *EPHESIANS 5:3-6* —

It is very important to know that whatever God has established, Satan will counterfeit. Where God establishes true love, Satan produces counterfeit love. God's love is unconditional and forgiving, looking for ways to heal the broken. But in our passage today, we see the world's love, and it is immoral, lustful, and self-indulgent. In this passage, not only does Paul warn against immoral actions but he also warns about immoral speech.

_____

"No one can serve two masters, for either he will hate the one and love the other,
or he will be devoted to the one and despise the other."

—Matthew 6:24

1 According to **Ephesians 5:3**, what sinful actions are we to avoid?

_____

_____

_____

2 **Ephesians 5:4a** gives instructions regarding our speech. What types of speech should we avoid?

To aid in your understanding, consider the following definitions:

- *Filthiness – general obscenity, cursing, and foul language*
- *Foolish talk – bragging or gloating about sinning*
- *Crude joking – turning words or innocent conversation into something obscene or suggestive*

_____

_____

_____

_____

_____

3 Instead of filthy and foolish talk, **Ephesians 5:4b** says our speech should be filled with thanksgiving. What are some of the things we should be thankful for according to the following verses?

1 Chronicles 16:8–12

_____

_____

_____

Psalm 28:7

_____

_____

_____

Psalm 86:12–13

_____

_____

_____

How long will we attribute thanksgiving (among other things) to God according to **Revelation 7:11–12**?

_____

_____

_____

_____

_____

_____

4 **Ephesians 5:5–6** are very strong verses and can be alarming to those who have committed sexual sin or covetousness. Remember what we learned in Lesson Five—for those who are in Jesus, our old selves are crucified with Christ, and we are new creatures in Jesus.

What else do you learn from the following verses?

Romans 8:1–2

_____

_____

_____

Romans 8:38–39

_____

_____

_____

1 John 1:9

_____

_____

_____

DAY 3
— READ EPHESIANS 5:7-14 —

"So you must live as God's obedient children. Don't slip back into your old ways of living to satisfy your own desires. You didn't know any better then. But now you must be holy in everything you do, just as God who chose you is holy. For the Scriptures say, "You must be holy because I am holy.""

—1 Peter 1:14–16 NLT

1 For those who know Jesus Christ as their Savior, we have moved from darkness into light. Record what you learn in **Ephesians 5:8–9**. Who are God's children now, and where is the fruit of light found?

_____

_____

_____

_____

2 Similarly, **Ephesians 5:1–2** tells us to imitate God and walk in love that He exemplified for us. What do the following verses say about this love?

Matthew 5:14–16

_____

_____

_____

John 8:12

_____

_____

_____

John 8:12

_____

_____

_____

3 As we have seen, the fruit of light is goodness and righteousness. Generally, goodness centers on our relationship with other people, and righteousness centers on our relationship with God. Using a dictionary (preferably a Bible dictionary, which you can find online if you do not own one), define these words:

Goodness

_____

_____

_____

Righteousness

_____

_____

_____

4 According to **Ephesians 5:10**, we are to discern what pleases the Lord. What are some things that please the Lord?

See the following verses for your answer.

Hosea 6:6

_____

_____

_____

Hebrews 11:6

_____

_____

_____

Hebrews 13:16

_____

_____

_____

5 Read **Ephesians 5:11–14.** What are we to do when we encounter evil deeds of darkness?

_____

_____

_____

6 What helpful thoughts are given regarding exposing sin in the following verses?

Matthew 7:3–5

_____

_____

_____

Matthew 18:15

_____

_____

_____

Galatians 6:1

_____

_____

_____

DAY 4
— READ *EPHESIANS 5:15–18* —

1 Read **Ephesians 5:15–18.** If you write in your Bible, circle the words *walk carefully* in the text. Then underline four key or instructive words or phrases—*as wise, best use, understand,* and *be filled.* If you prefer, write out the verses on an index card, and follow these directions.

You can put the index card in a visible spot to remind you of how to walk carefully.

2

What are Paul's instructions in **Ephesians 5:15** regarding our walk?

_____

_____

_____

What two types of people are contrasted?

_____

_____

According to **Ephesians 5:16**, why should we make the best use of our time?

_____

_____

_____

3

How does someone grow in wisdom according to these verses?

Proverbs 9:9–10

_____

_____

_____

Proverbs 13:20

_____

_____

_____

James 1:5

_____

_____

_____

4

I have heard it said that knowing God's will is easy. It is found in His Word, and all we need to do is read our Bibles. His will is always clear. In contrast, it is His *plan* that we sometimes struggle to know. With questions such as who we should marry, if we should take a certain job, where we should live, and more, it sometimes seems much more difficult to discern God's leading. Those answers are found in prayer, seeking the Lord, and waiting for His answer.

How do the following verses help you seek to know the will of God?

Psalm 119:105

_____

_____

_____

Psalm 119:129–130

_____

_____

_____

Romans 12:1–2

_____

_____

_____

As I have reflected on our questions today, I was convicted by **Ephesians 5:16**, which said to make "the best use of the time." That phrase, "the best use" has lingered in my mind.

It doesn't say the "good use of the time"; it says the best use.

How has God spoken to you today?

_____

_____

_____

_____

How will you make the best use of the time God has given you?

_____

_____

_____

_____

A MATTER OF PRAYER

As I stated earlier, we aren't going to skip the tough verses. Ephesians 5:18 may be easy for you, or it may cause you some struggles. It might even make you fall into judging others. I am simply going to give you my thoughts. Whatever your stance is on drinking alcohol, the Bible clearly states that drunkenness is wrong. On the issue of drinking itself, the Bible doesn't state exactly what we should do.

I asked my pastor, Gregg Matte, for some wise words to aid in deciding the issue of drinking alcohol. He said that as we decide what we are going to practice in this area, we must ask ourselves three questions: Does it hurt my walk with Christ? Does it hurt my witness for Christ? Does it hurt anyone else's walk with Christ? In Pastor Gregg's book *I AM Changes Who I Am*, he wrote, "For the believer in Christ, drinking is a prayerful decision to make before the Lord. Take your decision to the Lord in prayer. Search the Scriptures, asking not what is permissible but what is best. First Corinthians 10:31 tells us, 'Whatever you eat or drink or whatever you do, do all to the glory of the Lord.'"[15]

I know what God has called me to do in this area, and I don't drink alcohol. God may have a different calling on your life, and that is okay, too. The question is, have you prayed about it and considered your decision before Him?

The question in this passage isn't to drink or not; it is to be filled or not. Being filled with the Holy Spirit means being controlled by the Holy Spirit, and we need that filling daily. To be filled means to be complete and fully satisfied. Are you allowing the Holy Spirit to be your complete and total satisfaction, or are you looking to another source for your satisfaction? That's the real question.

DAY 5
— READ *EPHESIANS 5:19-21* —

When we are filled with His Spirit, this passage tells us two attitudes will spill from us: joy and thankfulness. Joy is being confident that God is in control of every situation and outcome we encounter, and thankfulness is recognizing that God is the giver of every good thing in our lives. Because of this, even in difficult times, we know that God can hold everything together and allows all things to work together for good. We can be confident of His power and His wisdom as we walk through tough times, knowing He will see us through. As we will see in our study today, joy and thanksgiving should flow from our hearts and characterize our relationship with God and with others.

1 How should we address one another according to **Ephesians 5:19**?

_____

_____

_____

_____

2 I have heard joy defined as "a deep experience of adequacy and confidence in spite of the circumstances around us." What do you learn about joy from the following verses?

Psalm 16:11

_____

_____

_____

Proverbs 17:22

_____

_____

_____

Jeremiah 15:16

_____

_____

_____

Romans 15:13

_____

_____

_____

According to **Ephesians 5:20**, how often are we to give thanks, and for what?

3

_____

_____

_____

"The word gratitude comes from the same root word as grace. If we have experienced the grace of God, then we ought to be grateful for what God brings to us. Thank and think also come from the same root word. If we would think more, we would thank more."[16]

—*Warren Wiersbe*

4

How often do we expect God to bless us and bless everything we do when we are often living in rebellion against some of God's rules? God's requirement is perfection, sinlessness, holiness, and righteousness, and what we deserve is death. But through His grace and provision by the death of His Son, we are offered life and given many good things despite our sin. An attitude of humility, joy, and thankfulness should automatically and permanently flow from our lives at all times. Read **Philippians 4:5–7** and write a prayer to God below that expresses your heart and thankfulness for all He has done for you.

_____

_____

_____

_____

5 As we prepare for our next lesson on submission, what do we learn in **Ephesians 5:21?**

_____

_____

_____

_____

Concluding Thoughts

Sometimes a lesson on living in purity can be tough. Of course, most of us are not living in the pigpen of sin, but let's face it; it is easy for us to excuse little sins. That's why we desperately need the Holy Spirit at work in our lives. And at the moment of salvation, the Holy Spirit begins His work in each of us. He teaches us about Jesus, helps us recall God's Word when we need it, intercedes for us in prayer before God, gives us the strength to lead godly lives, and convicts us of sin.

As we have seen in our study, we are commanded to be filled with the Holy Spirit. Remember, He is sealed inside of you, so He is always there. But the idea of allowing Him to fill you is different. Through the Holy Spirit, we have the power of God and the mind of Christ, and the entire basket of the fruit of His Spirit (see **Galatians 5:22–23**) all at our disposal, but how much of it do we actually appropriate?

I have been pondering the idea of filling, and the picture that keeps coming to my mind is a banquet table. The host steps forward and tells us all to eat our fill—the idea of eating until we are completely satisfied. If we think of filling as consuming until we are completely satisfied, then being filled with His Spirit is allowing Him to satisfy us until we need nothing else. We acknowledge that we need Him to be in control of everything we do, and apart from Him, we can do absolutely nothing. We do not care what the world thinks, but instead, we live to please God, looking for ways to draw others to Christ and glorify Christ in everything.

Once we are filled completely with Him, we step into this dark world to be light, living in a way that shows others we are different and that we belong to Jesus. When we are filled with the Holy Spirit, our thoughts and actions are controlled by Him, and our lives can overflow with joy, gratitude, and servant-heartedness marked with goodness, righteousness, and truth. We will be able to rightly expose the deeds of darkness and speak the truth truly in love.

I read a story about a miner who was lost in a dark mine and not sure where he was going. He was bumping into walls, following dark corridors and tunnels, and becoming more and more lost. Finally, in the distance, he saw a bit of faint light shining. He walked toward that light and found his way out of the mine. It was just a small bit of light shining forth that brought him freedom and life.

We are called to be that light shining in the darkness to a lost world, walking as children of the light and offering freedom and life through the message of the gospel of Jesus Christ. It requires a choice—to live in His way or in the way of the world. Which do you choose?

Additional Notes

_____
_____
_____
_____
_____
_____
_____
_____
_____
_____
_____
_____
_____
_____
_____
_____
_____
_____
_____
_____
_____
_____

LESSON SEVEN

Submission

— EPHESIANS 5:22–6:9 —

In our study, we have been talking about how our lives should look different from those outside the Christian faith. We should be walking in a manner worthy of Christ as God's children; we should react to others and situations in godly wisdom. The way we live our lives should be evidence to others that we are different, that we are holy because we belong to Jesus. We should be imitating Christ, walking as children of the light, and displaying His love and grace to others. Living this way requires a choice: to live in His way or in the way of the world.

There is a word that, in my opinion, sums up every lesson in this study, if not our daily Christian journey. That word is *surrender*. We must acknowledge that we need God in everything and in every part of our lives and that apart from Him, we can do nothing.

As we look at submission, you may need to surrender some societal ideas you may have been holding onto and trust that God knows best as He orders our world. We are going to address submission, and I hope that when we have completed this chapter, you will be thankful for God's line of authority in this area.

For me, I have simply looked at the idea of submission as being under an umbrella. I am under the umbrella of my husband and the umbrella of God. I can choose to walk out from underneath that umbrella, but I am going to experience the rain and get wet! The idea of submission is God's protection for me as His child. Can I make my own choices? Sure. Can I choose to be my own boss? Of course. Can I choose to do things my way? Most definitely. But when I do, I expose myself to the consequences of my choices and forfeit the protection God has set up for me. I may not always like the umbrella, but I'm grateful for it!

In this passage in Ephesians, Paul talks about submission in the context of marriage, but the concepts can be applied to any situation. As we saw in **Ephesians 5:21**, we are to submit to one another. You may not have a spouse, but it does not mean this lesson is not for you. There are plenty of relationships in your life that will benefit from the biblical truths of submitting to others in love.

This might be a difficult section of Scripture for you to study. Some parts of Scripture are harder than others to work through, understand, and apply, but we do not avoid the hard sections. We pray that God will give us understanding. We remain teachable, and we dive in.

DAY 1
— READ *EPHESIANS 5:21-24* —

1 Read **Ephesians 5:21–22**. Who is told to submit in this verse, and who are they to submit to?

_____
_____
_____

2 Read **Ephesians 5:23–24**. Who is the example for this relationship, and how is it described?

_____
_____
_____

3 Submission does not mean inferiority in relationships. Remember, on earth Christ is in submission to God the Father, and Christ is not inferior because of His submission. Wives are to submit to their husbands as an expression of their willing submission to the Lord. It is a picture to the world of the relationship of Christ to His church. What do the following verses say about the relationship between God and Jesus and the authority of Christ?

John 5:19–23

_____
_____
_____

John 8:28–29

_____
_____
_____

1 Corinthians 11:3

_____

_____

_____

Colossians 1:17–20

_____

_____

_____

How does **1 Peter 3:1–4** add to your understanding?

_____

_____

_____

_____

_____

_____

Proverbs 31:10–31 describes a virtuous woman in the eyes of God. What characteristics do you see in these verses?

_____

_____

_____

_____

_____

I love looking at the **Proverbs 31** woman. She is industrious and respected. She makes decisions, and she is gracious, generous, and a valuable wife and mother. Why not write a prayer to God thanking Him for the traits listed that you have seen in a godly woman in your life or traits you would like to see God develop in you?

_____

_____

_____

_____

_____

DAY 2
— READ *EPHESIANS 5:25-27* —

1 According to **Ephesians 5:25a**, what are husbands to do?

_____

_____

_____

2 Looking to Christ's love for the church as the example, what did Jesus do for the church according to **Ephesians 5:25b–27**?

_____

_____

_____

_____

3 While the Gospels provide many details describing Jesus' works and love for people, I think there is also an excellent summary in **Isaiah 61**. Just remember, the picture of Jesus is prophetic, which means it was written about Jesus before He came to earth, born of a virgin. It is a beautiful portrait of what the work of Jesus Christ would accomplish through His life, death, and resurrection.

What do you learn in the following verses from Isaiah?

Isaiah 61:1

_____

_____

_____

Isaiah 61:2

_____

_____

_____

Isaiah 61:3

_____

_____

_____

Isaiah 61:10

_____

_____

_____

4 Review the list you made from the question above. Which of Jesus Christ's actions is particularly meaningful to you? Why?

_____

_____

_____

_____

_____

5 Jesus' work is also beautifully summarized in the New Testament. Record what you read in **Philippians 2:5–11**.

_____

_____

_____

_____

_____

"Husbands, love your wives." Simple, huh? Well, yes and no. Your initial response is probably, "Of course, I love my wife. But then comes the qualifier, "Love your wives . . . just as Christ loved the church." Whoa. Now that's a whole other matter. To that you say, "How did Christ love the church?" And the Bible says, "He gave Himself up for her." Now notice that it does not say Christ gave of Himself. It says "He gave Himself."

How did Christ love the church? By giving. Christ's attitude toward the church—His bride—was one of total sacrifice. He . . .

> gave His time . . . the church was His number one priority
> gave His presence . . . He didn't send memos; He sent Himself
> gave His truth . . . to set us free
> gave His love . . . to meet our needs
> gave His prayers . . . to the Father for us
> gave His forgiveness . . . for our restoration
> gave His leadership . . . for our direction
> gave His inheritance . . . sharing with us His wealth and power
> Ultimately, of course, He gave His life.

All that Christ had and all that He was, He directed to the welfare of His bride, the church. Husband, if you love your wife as Christ loved the church, you must focus your entire life on her welfare and the welfare of your relationship with her. You must . . .

> give your time . . . she is your number one priority
> give your presence . . . both your physical and emotional presence
> give truth . . . take spiritual leadership in the home, making sure your wife and family are learning the truth
> give your love . . . to meet her needs
> give your prayers . . . to the Father for her tender care
> give your forgiveness . . . to restore the relationship
> give your leadership . . . for the home and family
> give your inheritance . . . sharing all that is yours with her

Often we think a husband loves his wife when he provides for her by bringing home a paycheck and buying the material things she needs. That is part of love, certainly, but it falls pitifully short of the standard Christ set in His love for the church. If that is as far as you have gotten as a husband, you barely have your big toe inside the door of biblical love.[17]

DAY 3
— READ *EPHESIANS 5:28-6:4* —

1 Paul continues with instructions to husbands. What does he say in **Ephesians 5:28, 31**, and **33a**? What additional instruction does he give to wives in **verse 33b**?

_____

_____

_____

2 What are some ways we can show honor and respect to one another according to the following verses?

Philippians 2:3

_____

_____

_____

Colossians 3:19

_____

_____

_____

1 Peter 3:7

_____

_____

_____

1 Peter 4:8–10

_____

_____

_____

3 What is Paul's instruction to children in **Ephesians 6:1–2**?

_____
_____
_____

4 What is the promise cited in **Ephesians 6:3**?

_____
_____
_____

Record this promise from the following verses:

Exodus 20:12

_____
_____
_____

Deuteronomy 5:32–33

_____
_____
_____

5 **Ephesians 6:4** tells us that fathers should not provoke their children to anger. How are parents to bring up their children according to this verse?

_____
_____
_____

"Sons and daughters still under their parents' roof are to obey and honor them. Obey has to do with action, and honor has to do with attitude. Although, as Paul has just mentioned, men and women are no longer under the authority of their parents once they themselves marry, . . . special respect and concern for their parents should continue as long as they live."[18]

—John MacArthur

DAY 4
— READ *EPHESIANS 6:5-8* —

Authority can be defined as the right to control, command, or determine derived from opinion, respect, or esteem; influence; a persuasive force; conviction; or commanding influence. The term *slaves* in the ancient East had a broad range of meanings. Frequently, a person would voluntarily place themselves under the authority of another as a slave or bondservant to pay off a debt or when they were under financial hardship. It is estimated that in Paul's day, a third of the Roman population were slaves. It was a common way of life.

For the questions below, you may find the questions easier to answer by using the New Living Translation below.

_____

Slaves, obey your earthly masters with deep respect and fear. Serve them sincerely as you would serve Christ. Try to please them all the time, not just when they are watching you. As slaves of Christ, do the will of God with all your heart. Work with enthusiasm, as though you were working for the Lord rather than for people. Remember that the Lord will reward each one of us for the good we do, whether we are slaves or free.

—Ephesians 6:5-8 NLT

1   Read **Ephesians 6:5-7**, which describes the relationship between a bondservant or slave and their earthly master. How does Paul instruct the servant to interact with their master? The principles in these verses could also be applied to an employee-employer relationship.

_____

_____

_____

_____

_____

2

What is the reminder given to everyone in **Ephesians 6:8**?

_____

_____

_____

_____

_____

3

In this passage, Paul has been telling those under someone's authority to work as if they were serving Christ and not man. In **Ephesians 6:9**, Paul instructs those in authority (masters) to treat those under them in the same way.

What is the reason for this according to **Ephesians 6:9b**?

_____

_____

_____

_____

_____

4

What do you learn about working in the following verses?

Proverbs 12:14

_____

_____

_____

Matthew 5:16

_____

_____

_____

Colossians 3:23–24

_____

_____

_____

Titus 3:1–2

_____

_____

_____

5 In yesterday's lesson, we saw that obedience has to do with action, and honor has to do with attitude. In evaluating situations where you are under the authority of another, how are your actions and attitudes toward that authority? How would you like to ask God to change your heart?

_____

_____

_____

DAY 5
— READ *EPHESIANS 6:9* —

Today we will focus on how to be a good employee or employer. Even if you do not work outside the home, you may serve on a committee or volunteer at church or somewhere else. All those things fall under a line of authority, and we are to serve and work just as if we were doing it for Jesus. Whether we are the authority or under an authority, we need to treat everyone with respect. None are inferior or superior because there is no partiality with God. We must treat everyone with respect because we are all equal in God's sight.

1 What does **Ephesians 6:9a** instruct masters to do? *For our application, we are applying the word master to an authority or boss.*

_____

_____

_____

2 The last sentence in **Ephesians 6:9** says that God does not show partiality or have favorites. How is that further explained in the following verses?

Job 13:10

_____

_____

_____

Romans 3:22–23

_____

_____

_____

James 2:1–9

_____

_____

_____

3 What does **Romans 13:1–2** say regarding our responsibility toward the government?

_____

_____

_____

_____

_____

4 While we may not politically agree with the governmental authority, what do we learn about God's role in directing government?

Proverbs 21:1

_____

_____

_____

Daniel 2:21

_____

_____

_____

5 Another passage of scripture that gives us instruction about submission is **1 Peter 2:13–18**. What do you learn from this passage?

_____

_____

_____

_____

_____

_____

It is important to note that while we are instructed to submit to earthly authorities in our lives such as a husband or a boss, our first responsibility is obedience to God. If an authority asks you to be disobedient to your Creator and Savior, choose to be obedient to God and His Word over the requests of a human being.

6. In what ways has God touched your heart in our study this week? Is there an area of your life you need to improve? Is there an attitude of your heart you need to change? Are you burdened to pray for another person? Why not write a prayer to God, pouring out what is in your heart and asking Him for the courage to obey and wisdom to walk worthy in submission?

_____

_____

_____

_____

Concluding Thoughts

We have made it through the lesson on submission—wives submitting to husbands, husbands sacrificially loving their wives, children obeying and honoring parents, and employees respecting employers. The thought-provoking question for you and me is this: To whom or what do you give authority in your life? In my life, I see God as my ultimate authority, but I also see my husband, my pastor, my women's minister, and the heads of several organizations I volunteer for as my authorities. While I would love to say I honor and willingly submit myself to those authorities every moment, if I am honest, the authority I bow before all too often is my own will and self-centeredness.

When you give authority to someone or something in your life, you are choosing to give them the right to control your actions or attitudes and determine the course of action for your life. Many times, if not most often, I would hope the one you trust and choose to control your life is Jesus Christ. I desire to always let God be in control of my life, but unfortunately, I don't always surrender my will completely to

Him. At times, all of us make other choices regarding who we want as our authority. Too often, we allow Satan to whisper defeating lies to us and find that we have turned our focus from Jesus to something else, allowing Satan's destructive falsehoods to become a persuasive influence over our decisions.

Sometimes those persuasive influences we allow to control us are the opinions of other people, maybe even people 20 years in our past. Those haunting words of the past or petty words of a naysayer from middle school can drive the decisions we make today. And right alongside those opinions is the demon of comparison. How often are we influenced by what we think others have that we are missing in our lives or use our judgmental opinion of others to try to inflate our opinion of ourselves? Comparison robs us of joy in life, and it is a terrible influencer!

We sometimes think we are more enlightened than God and know better how to choose the path for our lives, and we push Jesus aside and try to do things on our own. And if I am really honest, sometimes what I choose to submit to is something as simple as a bag of potato chips that calls to me from the darkness of the pantry and leads me down an evil road!

We are also very quick to let created things—TV, computer, phone, social media, or even bad habits—have far too much importance in our lives. When we give them too much significance or spend too much time comparing ourselves online to our circle of friends, they are controlling us. Unfortunately, we all too often succumb to the pressure to turn our attention and affection toward these things.

The commanding influence of our lives must be Jesus.

He is the ultimate authority.

Additional Notes

_____

_____

_____

_____

_____

_____

_____

LESSON EIGHT

Spiritual Warfare

— EPHESIANS 6:10-24 —

There is a battle raging between the spiritual forces of good and the spiritual forces of evil. It began before the creation of the world, continued throughout the ages, and will not be over until time has found its end. Satan desires to be worshiped and wants to usurp anything that belongs to God. He wants mankind to turn their attention and affection away from God. From the time you are born, there is a battle for your soul. Once you have chosen Jesus as your Savior and your eternity is secure, then the battle is for your heart and your mind.

Satan wants you to take your eyes off Jesus, just as Peter did as he was walking on the water. He wants to defeat you, cause you to stumble, and cause your Christian walk to get off track. He wants you to fall into sin and destroy your life. He wants to destroy your fellowship with God, your relationships with others, your reputation, and your faith.

Satan is a counterfeiter. He will take what is bad and make it look good. He will somehow make wrong things look like they are right. He distorts the truth and makes sin that will destroy us look like fun. He misleads, misdirects, and misinforms us.

While sometimes we can see Satan coming (he is described in **1 Peter 5:8** as a roaring lion), he is also very crafty and sneaky and will disguise himself as an angel of light (**2 Corinthians 11:14**). We have to stand strong against the schemes of the devil. We have to be prepared for the battle.

DAY 1
— READ EPHESIANS 6:10-12 —

1

Read **Ephesians 6:10**. What does Paul tell us to do in this verse?

_____

_____

_____

_____

_____

_____

2   Read the following verses, and record what you learn about God's strength.

Psalm 18:1–3

_____
_____
_____

Psalm 50:1–2

_____
_____
_____

Proverbs 18:10

_____
_____
_____

3   According to **Ephesians 6:12**, what or who are we battling against?

_____
_____
_____
_____
_____

4   What do the following verses say about God's authority and power over Satan?

Romans 16:20

_____
_____
_____

1 John 3:8

_____
_____
_____

Revelation 20:10

_____
_____
_____

5 What do these verses say about our victory in warfare?

1 Corinthians 15:57

_____

_____

_____

1 John 5:4–5

_____

_____

_____

6 The passage in **1 John 4:4** reminds us that Jesus who lives in us is greater than Satan who lives in the world. We have power over Satan who is a defeated foe. Can you recall a time when you recognized a scheme Satan had planned against you and stood firm in your faith?

_____

_____

_____

DAY 2
— READ *EPHESIANS 6:12* —

According to the Book of Revelation, Satan is defeated by Jesus in the Battle of Armageddon and eventually thrown into the Lake of Fire where he will suffer torment forever. Even though his demise is certain, it is important to understand that while Satan will be cast down at the end of time, he has been given temporary power to rule on earth. While earth might be his temporary kingdom until Jesus returns, he is still weak compared to the strength of God who lives in us. We are victorious now over Satan. Don't forget that! However, it is also important to know our foe so we recognize his attacks on us.

1 Before we were created, Satan was called Lucifer, or the Morning Star. He was an angel living in heaven. **Ezekiel 28:13–19** and **Isaiah 14:12–15** record his sin and how God cast him from heaven. What do you learn in these passages? What would you consider to be Satan's main offense?

_____

_____

_____

_____

_____

2 What do the following verses say about pride?

Psalm 31:23

_____

_____

_____

Proverbs 11:2

_____

_____

_____

Proverbs 16:18

_____

_____

_____

1 John 2:16

_____

_____

_____

3 What do the following verses say about Satan?

Job 1:7

_____

_____

_____

1 Peter 5:8

_____

_____

_____

2 Corinthians 11:14

_____

_____

_____

Revelation 12:9–10

_____

_____

_____

4   According to **John 10:10**, what is Satan's goal? What does Jesus promise us?

_____

_____

_____

_____

_____

5   What encouragement do you find in the following verses?

Psalm 91:3–16

_____

_____

_____

James 4:7

_____

_____

_____

Revelation 12:7–8

_____

_____

_____

DAY 3
— READ *EPHESIANS 6:13-14* —

As we look at the armor of God over the next two days, it is critical to understand the protection God has provided you. We will look at each piece individually, but we are commanded to put on the whole armor of God—every single piece. We do not get to pick and choose. Anything you leave off will leave you vulnerable to attack. And if you give Satan even the smallest foothold in your life, he will set out to eventually wreak havoc on your entire life.

1

Read **Ephesians 6:13**. What are we commanded to do, and why?

_____
_____
_____
_____

2

Read **Ephesians 6:14**. What are the pieces of armor listed in this verse?

_____
_____
_____
_____

3

The Belt of Truth can have several meanings, but I have heard it best defined as knowing the truth of Christ and acting on it by living in integrity. In our modern world of no absolutes and the idea of believing whatever seems right to you, girding ourselves in the truth found in Jesus is critical. We must know and act on the truth.

What do you learn about truth from the following verses?

John 1:17

_____
_____
_____

John 8:31–32

_____

_____

_____

John 14:6

_____

_____

_____

4   What does **John 8:44** say about Satan?

_____

_____

_____

5   What do the following verses say about the righteousness of Christ?

Romans 5:17–18

_____

_____

_____

Philippians 3:9

_____

_____

_____

6   Compare the verses above with **Isaiah 64:6** that speaks of the righteousness we achieve on our own. Write a prayer of thanksgiving, thanking God that by His grace through salvation we exchange our righteousness for the righteousness of Christ.

Hallelujah!

_____

_____

_____

_____

_____

DAY 4
— READ EPHESIANS 6:15–17 —

Shield of Faith

In biblical days, shields were made of wood and were designed to be interlocked. In battle, a battalion of men could hook their shields together and march into enemy fire. What a beautiful picture and reminder that we are not alone in our battle. How often does Satan lie to us that we are all alone? He convinces us that no one else has ever experienced what we are going through and that no one could understand us.

Galatians 6:2 tells us that we should carry each other's burdens. When we are struggling, in a difficult situation, or are overwhelmed with life, share your burden with those in the faith who can stand with you. They will fight battles alongside you, encouraging you and lifting you up.

Even more encouraging is the truth found in Deuteronomy 31:8 that says, "It is the Lord who goes before you. He will be with you; he will not leave you or forsake you. Do not fear or be dismayed." God is with you always—in every battle, in every circumstance, in every moment, He is there.

Oh, friend, you are never alone!

1

Read **Ephesians 6:15–17**. What do you learn about the following pieces of your armor?

Shoes

_____

_____

_____

Shield of faith

_____

_____

_____

Sword of the Spirit

_____

_____

_____

2

Our battle shoes indicate a readiness for battle and standing firm in confidence. What do the following verses say?

Deuteronomy 31:6

_____

_____

_____

Proverbs 3:25–26

_____

_____

_____

3

The Shield of Faith is a picture of the saints linking together in battle. Consider this picture as you read **Luke 5:17–20**, a beautiful story about a man's friends helping him when he was in need. What do you learn from this story? What happened on account of their faith?

_____

_____

_____

4

It has been said that if Satan can influence our minds, he can control our hearts. What do we learn about our minds from the following verses?

Romans 12:2

_____

_____

_____

Philippians 4:7

_____

_____

_____

5 What do you learn about the Word of God from the following verses?

Psalm 119:159–160

_____

_____

_____

John 17:17

_____

_____

_____

Hebrews 4:12

_____

_____

_____

DAY 5

— READ *EPHESIANS 6:18-24* —

In **Ephesians 6**, we learn about the armor of God and are given two offensive weapons to take into battle with us. Yesterday we looked at the sword of the Spirit (the Word of God). Today's focus will be on our other weapon: prayer. It is important to look at prayer separately; it is like the air we must continually breathe.

"Prayer is the closing theme of Ephesians, and though it is closely related to God's armor, it is not mentioned as a part of it, because it is much more than that. Prayer is not merely another godly weapon, as important as those weapons are. All the while that we are fighting in the girdle of truth, the breastplate of righteousness, the shoes of the gospel of peace, the shield of faith, the helmet of salvation, and the sword of the Spirit, we are to be in prayer. Prayer is the very spiritual air that the soldier of Christ breathes. It is the all-pervasive strategy in which warfare is fought."[19]

—John MacArthur

1. According to **Ephesians 5:3**, what sinful actions are we to avoid?

   _____
   _____
   _____
   _____

2. Look up the word *supplication* in a dictionary, and write the definition below.

   _____
   _____
   _____
   _____

3

What do the following verses say about supplication?

Philippians 4:6

_____
_____
_____

1 Timothy 2:1–3

_____
_____
_____

4

Ephesians 6:18 also tells us to persevere in making supplication for others. Look up the word _persevere_, and write the definition below.

_____
_____
_____
_____
_____

5

Can you recall a time when you persevered in making supplication for another?

_____
_____
_____
_____
_____
_____

6

Psalm 62:8 tells us that God is trustworthy and we can pour out our hearts before Him. As we conclude our study for this week, thank Him that He is trustworthy, and then trust Him as you pour out the things from your heart that are concerning you today.

_____
_____
_____
_____
_____
_____

"Tell God all that is in your heart, as one unloads one's heart, its pleasures and its pains, to a dear friend. Tell Him your troubles, that He may comfort you; tell Him your joys, that He may sober them; tell Him your longings, that He may purify them; tell Him your dislikes, that He may help you to conquer them; talk to Him of your temptations, that He may shield you from them; show Him the wounds of your heart, that He may heal them; lay bare your indifference to good, your depraved tastes for evil, your instability. Tell Him how self-love makes you unjust to others, how vanity tempts you to be insincere, how pride disguises you to yourself as to others." [20]

—Chuck Swindoll

Concluding Thoughts

While Satan is a crafty, manipulative creature, you can have victory over him. Through Jesus, Satan no longer has power over you. You possess all the resources of God to overcome and free you from any attempt of Satan to entangle you. So how do you overcome the evil one?

1. Be alert to all of Satan's tricks. Satan wants to catch you by surprise, so make every effort to evaluate what the adversary is doing. Watch out for temptation because when you are prepared for his attempts to mislead you, you will not be vulnerable to his ways. Our command is to resist him, and he will flee (**James 4:7**). Also, be on the lookout for false teachers. Satan is a liar who disguises himself as an angel of light and tries to mislead by using the Word of God and distorting its truth. Study God's Word carefully, diligently, and faithfully.

2. Be firm in your faith, rooted and grounded in God's Word. Establish that God is the authority for your life, and look to no others. Lean on God, His Son, and the power of the resurrection, and make sure you are grounded in sound doctrine.

3. Grow in your maturity as a believer in Christ. If you are busy with childish things, you cannot defend yourself against the antics of Satan. Commit to obeying God's truth (**1 Peter 2:2**), and don't settle for a shallow knowledge of God's Word.

4. Be strong in your resolve to stand against Satan. Do not allow your flesh to rule, and exercise self-control. As **Ephesians 3:16** says, yield to the Spirit of God, and you will be strengthened by His strength. God provides strength as you practice discipline and self-control rather than yielding to the ways of the world.

My mother was a wise and godly woman. Not only was she an amazing Bible teacher, but she also was a brilliant Christian counselor. When I was struggling with defeating situations and trying to combat the lies of Satan with the truth of God's Word, she gave me a simple phrase to use to help me keep my eyes on the truth. She told me to say, "because I am a child of God."

When I felt like a failure because of a mistake I had made, she reminded me to say that simple phrase after I stated my feelings. For example, I would say, "I am a failure because I am a child of God." If the sentence did not make any sense spiritually, then I knew it was a lie, and I would release those thoughts. I am not a failure because I am a child of God; in fact, I am just the opposite. I am a conqueror (**Romans 8:37**)

I think about my mom often. She passed away many years ago from ovarian cancer, and I miss her every day. There are times that I wish I could share my thoughts and ideas with her, get her advice, and just hear her voice again. Just this week I was reminded of the verses in **Hebrews 12:1–2** that say, "Therefore, since we are surrounded by so great a cloud of witnesses, let us also lay aside every weight, and the sin which clings so closely, and let us run with endurance the race that is set before us, looking to Jesus, the founder and perfecter of our faith, who for the joy that was set before him endured the cross, despising the shame, and is seated at the right hand of the throne of God."

In **Hebrews 11**, Paul reminds us of all the faithful saints who have lived before us and are now in heaven. While my mom is not listed in Hebrews (of course), she was a faithful saint as well. I know she is waiting for me in heaven cheering me on, and although I cannot see her, I know she is part of the cloud of faithful witnesses who surround me on my journey. What an encouragement to run on!

And you should be encouraged too. You are surrounded by a cloud of witnesses—your family, amazing friends, godly mentors, and your heavenly Father who promises to never leave you or forsake you. Stand firm in your protective armor, knowing you have an army who stands with you and a God who fights for you!

Additional Notes

_____
_____
_____
_____
_____
_____
_____
_____
_____
_____
_____
_____
_____
_____
_____
_____
_____
_____
_____
_____
_____
_____
_____
_____
_____

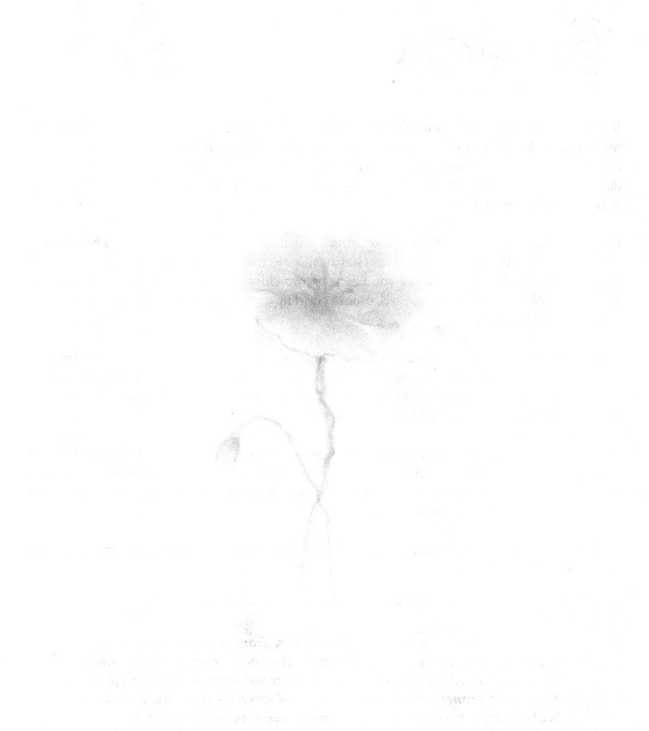

Benediction

It is my prayer that as you conclude this study, you have a better understanding of just how much you are loved by God. I hope you have come to see that you have been greatly blessed, but with that blessing also comes the responsibility to live your life in thankfulness and holiness, depending upon the Holy Spirit to live through you as you find your satisfaction, not in the things of this world but in God alone.

Don't let Satan ever rob you of the joy of knowing that you are loved and accepted by the God who spoke the universe into existence. God is all-powerful, all-knowing, holy, gracious, and forgiving, and He has chosen to call you His very own child. He invites you to have a personal, deep relationship with Him. You are welcome to crawl up on His lap as His child. He's your Daddy God, your Abba Father.

Never let the lies of Satan convince you of anything else. You are worthy of His love, not because of anything you have done but because Jesus makes you worthy. He makes you new. He forgives your sin and makes you stand holy and righteous before God in the righteousness of Jesus Christ. You have been redeemed by the blood of Jesus.

If you don't know Jesus in this personal way, it is my prayer that you come to know Him and experience the freedom that His death on the cross has purchased for you. He has given you a gift of salvation, but it is up to you whether you will claim the gift as your own or walk away. If He's calling you, don't wait. One day it will be too late.

I can think of no better way to end our study than with this prayer I am praying for you now from **Ephesians 3:14–21 (NET).**

For this reason, I kneel before the Father, from whom every family in heaven and on earth is named. I pray that according to the wealth of His glory He will grant you to be strengthened with power through His Spirit in the inner person, that Christ will dwell in your hearts through faith, so that, because you have been rooted and grounded in love, you will be able to comprehend with all the saints what is the breadth and length and height and depth, and thus to know the love of Christ that surpasses knowledge, so that you will be filled up to all the fullness of God.

Now to Him who by the power that is working within us is able to do far beyond all that we ask or think, to Him be the glory in the church and in Christ Jesus to all generations, forever and ever. Amen.

Notes

1   Warren Wiersbe, *Be Rich* (Colorado Springs, Co: David C. Cook, 2004), 18.

2   John MacArthur, *The MacArthur New Testament Commentary: Ephesians* (Chicago: Moody Publishers, 1986), 11.

3   Spiros Zodhiates, T*he Complete Word Study New Testament* (Chattanooga, TN: AMG Publishers, 1991), 967.

4   Warren Wiersbe, *Be Rich* (Colorado Springs, CO: David C. Cook, 2004), 40.

5   John MacArthur, *The MacArthur New Testament Commentary: Ephesians* (Chicago: Moody Publishers, 1986), 63.

6   Warren Wiersbe, *Be Rich* (Colorado Springs, CO: David C. Cook, 2004), 32.

7   Warren Wiersbe, *Be Rich* (Colorado Springs, CO: David C. Cook, 2004), 82.

8   John MacArthur, *The MacArthur New Testament Commentary: Ephesians* (Chicago: Moody Publishers, 1986), 116.

9   John MacArthur, *The MacArthur New Testament Commentary: Ephesians* (Chicago: Moody Publishers, 1986), 124.

10   "A Radical Change," *Ray Stedman*, accessed January 26, 2022, https://www.raystedman.org/daily-devotions/ephesians/a-radical-change.

11   "A Radical Change," *Ray Stedman*, accessed January 26, 2022, https://www.raystedman.org/daily-devotions/ephesians/a-radical-change.

12   John MacArthur, *The MacArthur New Testament Commentary: Ephesians* (Chicago: Moody Publishers, 1986), 181.

13   "Be Godlike," *Ray Stedman*, accessed January 26, 2022, https://www.raystedman.org/daily-devotions/ephesians/be-godlike.

14   John MacArthur, *The MacArthur New Testament Commentary: Ephesians* (Chicago: Moody Publishers, 1986), 195.

15   Gregg Matte, *I AM Changes Who I Am* (Grand Rapids, MI: Baker Books, 2012), 207.

16   Warren Wiersbe, *Be Rich* (Colorado Springs, CO: David C. Cook, 2004), 141.

17   Max Anders, *The Good Life* (New York: W Pub Group, 1993).

18   John MacArthur, *The MacArthur New Testament Commentary: Ephesians* (Chicago: Moody Publishing, 1986), 311.

19   John MacArthur, *The MacArthur New Testament Commentary: Ephesians* (Chicago: Moody Publishing, 1986), 377.

20   Pastor Chuck Swindoll, "Praying to Your Friend," *Insight for Living*, accessed January 26, 2022, https://insight.org/resources/daily-devotional/individual/praying-to-your-friend1.

CPSIA information can be obtained
at www.ICGtesting.com
Printed in the USA
LVHW021050030822
725067LV00007B/180